Ego and Self

Marie-Louise von Franz, Honorary Patron

**Studies in Jungian Psychology
by Jungian Analysts**

Daryl Sharp, General Editor

EGO AND SELF
The Old Testament Prophets

— From Isaiah to Malachi —

EDWARD F. EDINGER
Transcribed and Edited by J. Gary Sparks

To Edward F. Edinger himself, who passed away before seeing this book in print. We hope he likes it, wherever he is. And to his gracious partner and fellow analyst, Dianne D. Cordic.

Canadian Cataloguing in Publication Data

Edinger, Edward F. (Edward Ferdinand), 1922-1998
  Ego and self: the Old Testament Prophets: from Isaiah to Malachi

(Studies in Jungian psychology by Jungian analysts; 90)

Includes bibliographical references and index.

ISBN 0-919123-91-0

1. Bible. O.T. Prophets—Psychology. 2. Bible. O.T. Prophets—Criticism, interpretaton, etc. 3. Individuation (Psychology). 4. Self.
5. Ego (Psychology. 6. Jungian psychology—Religious aspects.
I. Sparks, J. Gary (John Gary), 1948- . II. Title. III. Series.

BS1286.E34 2000   224'.001'9   C00-930272-7

INNER CITY BOOKS
Box 1271, Station Q, Toronto, Canada M4T 2P4

Telephone (416) 927-0355 / Fax (416) 924-1814
E-mail: icb@inforamp.net / Web site: www.innercitybooks.net

Honorary Patron: Marie-Louise von Franz.
Publisher and General Editor: Daryl Sharp.
Senior Editor: Victoria Cowan.

INNER CITY BOOKS was founded in 1980 to promote the understanding and practical application of the work of C.G. Jung.

Cover: A malacate, or spindle whorl, in *Designs from Pre-Columbian Mexico,* ed. Jorge Enciso (New York: Dover Publications, 1971).

Index by Victoria Cowan

Printed and bound in Canada by University of Toronto Press Incorporated

Contents

See final page for other books by Edward F. Edinger

Illustrations

Source credits are given in the captions

Edward F. Edinger, 1922-1998

Editor's Foreword

Jungian psychology is a distillation of the reactions from unconscious spheres to conscious experience. It is a record of life's spontaneous emotional fire searing its purposes onto human hearts and minds. It is an attempt to let the patterns in our sweltering turbulence show their meaningful face.

How profoundly that fire and amplitude lived for Edward F. Edinger. I find in all aspects of his work such nearness to heartfelt images as characterized C.G. Jung's own passionate genius. The intensity of Edinger's creativity expresses exactly the fervent richness of the unconscious's response to modern life. Throughout his authorship and in an unpretentious style brimming with feeling and care, Edinger has powerfully put forward for us the main features of today's complexity, psychologically seen: the dark side of God, the transformation of central values, a possible meaning in social fragmentation, the self-centered euphoria of our age, varied images of transformation at depth—to name a few. His exceptional grasp of our experience and its background bears indisputable witness to the integrity of this man's consistently creative flame.

In the pages which follow Edward Edinger once more turns his ardent and discerning mind to a theme of acute importance for our era: the wider nature of symbolic processes.

One of Jung's enduring accomplishments is to have established that the apparently random images in our dreams and fantasies are in fact highly coherent symbols. When we seek to understand the messages of these symbols, the inherent wisdom within our personality is demonstrated to us, Jung could clearly show. Dreams and fantasies are not senseless happenings; they are meaningful psychological occurrences capable of conveying through their picture-language a knowledge of who we are and how our lives are purposefully to develop. Although Jung first located the symbol-creating capacity to lie within each individual, expressed most typically in night dreams and day-dreaming, he soon saw this formulation was inadequate to explaining the real nature of symbols. He had found certain facts which contradicted a merely subjective appraisal of them and how they work.

His observation of the phenomenon he called synchronicity challenged his initial thesis. In a synchronistic incident symbolic images which we know from our inner world appear, it would seem, in events of the outer world. Symbols do not merely occur "inside" us, in other words. Apparently events in the outer world, concrete physical events, also behave symbolically, insofar as an outer event—resonating with an image we know from our inner work—at times repeats a theme we have just become aware of in our subjective experience. The image-producing capacity of the personality does not merely lie inside us, then: it also seems to extend to the physical matter of outer reality. This indeed goes against Jung's original idea that symbols are mere "psychological" processes. It also—as Jung well knew—certainly goes against the predominant view of physical science which holds that matter is inert and without rational purpose.

In his address at the 1948 founding of the C.G. Jung Institute in Zürich, Jung discussed how he hoped future research into his psychology would develop. At the top of his list was this issue: what is the relation between symbols and matter—or, as he put it, between psyche and matter? His point likewise leads us to acknowledge several related questions. How does taking the confluence between psyche and matter seriously challenge us to review our understanding of both symbols and the material world? How is our inner psychology also part of the outer physical world, and vice-versa? What does the hidden unity between inside and outside mean for us and the way we live our lives? How will our values which so carefully keep the inner and outer worlds apart have to change as the distinction we make between the two is known to be false? What will become of our view of life which essentially sees material events as random and without purpose when the veil is lifted from happenstance as a frame of reference?

Edward Edinger's work on the Old Testament prophets takes up in an illuminating fashion this challenge of the link between symbol and matter, that is, between the inner world and outer world, and his work thus again stands directly in the mainstream of creative Jungian research. Edinger's discussion turns to a time when symbol and matter—the locus of revealed meaning and concrete historical events—were not separated. For the Old Testament prophets, the physical circumstances of history were connected with deeper—actually, the deepest—significance. The intention of Yahweh was manifest directly in the vicissitudes of Israel's history and was to be read through them. The prophets' idiom is a sacred one, of course, and analytical psychology proceeds from different foundations. But still we can take our cue from this ancient time and examine its understanding of meaning when symbol and episode are as yet not disconnected. Edinger beautifully makes the translation, for the modern reader, from the Hebrew interpretation of history as manifestations of divine significance to the language of depth psychology, which empirically documents symbolic intelligence in the material events of daily living. The lens of analytical psychology, here in the hands of the seasoned practitioner, affords the opportunity to investigate the phenomena of life when they are seen in their wider perspective.

The points Edinger raises and describes in his deep-hearted way are important for both layperson and professional to consider. What is a symbolic event and how does it take place in the history of a person or group? How does a mature individual understand his or her place in this historical process? How is an historical awareness an integral part of full living? What typical symbolic images accompany those incidents in the outer world which communicate to an individual their unique purpose in life? What do images of the unconscious manifesting in outer reality look like in the first place? What is to be recognized as general and historical in apparently personal and emotional reactions, and how are we to work with them analytically? In what way is it possible for an individual to live out the larger experience of the times in their specifically subjective reactions? What of these subjective reactions are expressions of the coming fate of a person's nation or culture? How is our own life and suffering ever to attain the dignity of expressing significance for our community, culture or historical period?

We live in a time of me, me and more me. We are obsessed with ourselves and seek to acquire more of what we already are so as to defend against the increasingly crushing brutality of a world that is at best callous and amoral. It certainly looks like the name of modern life is "me versus the world." But as the Old Testament prophets have shown and as Edinger reinterprets, it is just possible that the world we feel so adversarial toward is also part of us, and that—in fact—we've got it all wrong. The most important part of ourselves may not only be inside us, but also outside. Pressing on us now is the need to recognize that in giving ourselves to matters on the outside, we are also giving to the essence of ourselves which we had thought was only on the inside, because often, if we know how to look, we will find our inside is really on the outside. The outer world can just as well reveal the symbolic nature of our life and destiny as can the inner.

I thank Edward Edinger for this work, and I am very happy to have had the opportunity to bring it to print. I particularly thank the author for his life-long devotion to demonstrating, through its own language, the full depth and breadth of the personality's extraordinary attempt to express who we are and where we are going, and so to heal us and our times.

J. Gary Sparks

Introduction
History As Sacred Scripture

I want to say a few words about the idea of history as sacred scripture. Up to now what we've been reading purports to be history, the history of Israel.[1] But this history is simultaneously Israel's mythology. Along with the political and military accounts that are presented we are also given a record of Yahweh's intervention in human affairs, of the dialogue between God and humanity. And that is one of the precious aspects of this text.

The same phenomenon is alluded to, just very briefly, fleetingly even, in Homer's *Iliad*. Although the Trojan War was historical, we have the picture of it as unfolding with an almost capricious, erratic intervention of the gods. There is just the mere beginning of the idea of a dialogue between God and man, but it is primitive in comparison to the highly sophisticated, differentiated, ongoing dialogue between Yahweh and the nation of Israel.

One of the things this record tells us when we consider it psychologically is that this is the nature of history in general. All history is a visible manifestation of God's engagement in human affairs, God on the human plane, so to speak. All history is that, but it is as though the Jews were the only ones who realized it—with their religious genius, their ability to perceive the transpersonal dimension working in the background.

In modern times the philosopher Hegel has given expression to this same idea. He said that history is the manifestation and unfolding in time of what he called the World Spirit—a sort of philosophical euphemism for God.[2] And he tells us that history is the visible manifestation of God which can occur only with the appearance of self-conscious man. Even more succinctly, he says that history is the autobiography of God. And we know psychologically that God needs history as his other, as his object. Hegel had a remarkable understanding of this overall phenomenon. And if one adds to his vision of things our own psychological understanding, we

---

[1] [This refers to Dr. Edinger's seminars on the historical books of the Old Testament (see below, p. 15), published as *The Bible and the Psyche: Individuation Symbolism in the Old Testament.*—Ed.]
[2] See *The Philosophy of History,* particularly the Introduction.

13

can then see that God's need for history and concrete realization is the basis of his need for humanity.

The way I would put it is that the entire human drama of recorded history is God's dream, whereby, once he begins investigating his dreams, he will start becoming conscious of himself. And that is something of the purpose of what Jung called the "miserable morass of human history."

If we think of collective history as meaningful, then we'll attribute the same level of importance to individual history. First of all to our own history, and secondly to the history of our patients. And that's why every careful analysis starts with a detailed history of the patient. I think of such a beginning as a reading of the scripture of that person's life. So I study an individual's history the same way I study the books of the Old Testament. Because that history, if you are open to it, can be perceived as a record of God's intervention in this person's life and as a dialogue between the Self and the developing ego. So I always try to be on the lookout for evidence of a transpersonal purpose in an individual's life story. Once you are on the lookout for such a thing, it becomes visible in everyone's life account.

The material we deal with in these lectures is dense. What you need is a ruminant stomach: take it all in and then digest it later, regurgitate it and chew the cud. That is the stomach of a ruminant. That is the principle I operate on. I know that what I throw out is impossible to digest all at once, so I hope you have ruminant stomachs. You see there is something ludicrous about covering such a mass of material in the course of a brief academic year. And yet if one doesn't make the effort . . . well, let me just say I'd rather make the effort than not. So I am going to plunge right in.

1
Isaiah, Part One

You may recall that one way of classifying or dividing the contents of the Old Testament is the threefold division of seventeen books of history, five books of wisdom and poetry, and seventeen books of the prophets, which may be listed as follows:

Historical	Poetical-Wisdom	Prophetic
Genesis	Job	Isaiah
Exodus	Psalms	Jeremiah
Leviticus	Proverbs	Lamentations
Numbers	Ecclesiastes	Ezekiel
Deuteronomy	Song of Solomon	Daniel
Joshua		Hosea
Judges		Joel
Ruth		Amos
1 Samuel		Obadiah
2 Samuel		Jonah
1 Kings		Micah
2 Kings		Nahum
1 Chronicles		Habakkuk
2 Chronicles		Zephaniah
Ezra		Haggai
Nehemiah		Zechariah
Esther		Malachi

By that classification we are starting the third category tonight in talking about Isaiah.

It is generally accepted that the Book of Isaiah was written by at least two authors. The original Isaiah lived in the eighth century B.C. and the so-called Deutero-Isaiah or Second Isaiah, who's thought to be the author of most of chapters 40-66, lived during or after the Babylonian exile. But they come down to us as a single book, most likely because of an underlying symbolic continuity. I think we'll find that continuity to derive basically from the preoccupation with the same archetypal image: the Messianic advent.

Tonight we'll be talking about the so-called First Isaiah, who is responsible for chapters 1-39, and who lived from approximately 760 B.C. to somewhere past 700. We don't know precisely. Anyway it was a time of terror, because the militaristic nation, Assyria, was rampaging through the Middle East, and Israel and Judah lived in perpetual danger of destruction by their aggressive armies.

I think we can understand the terror of the times to be at least partly responsible for the activation of Isaiah's unconscious. Though understandable on the surface as reactions to the threat of Assyria, when viewed psychologically we can see the archetypal psyche activated by the urgency of the circumstances. Isaiah's visions and prophecies therefore took on a universal relevance. They became an expression of archetypal reality, archetypal danger and archetypal rescue. That can be demonstrated as we examine the chief images contained in his message.

Isaiah is certainly a most remarkable individual. Not the least of his notable qualities was indicated in the description of his call, which is described in the sixth chapter where he is just sort of eavesdropping on Yahweh and hears that the Lord needs somebody. Isaiah says, "Here I am, send me." (6:8)[3] That's almost unique among the prophetic calls, that degree of willingness; it certainly is in sharp contrast to Moses' reaction.

At any rate he had remarkable experiences of the unconscious, and out of those experiences crystalized several basic images of the Western psyche. The three chief images I want to talk about, really different aspects of the same core image, are the image of the Day of Yahweh, the image of the righteous remnant that survives the Day of Yahweh, and the image of the Messiah and the Messianic banquet that is part of the coming of the Messiah.

The Day of Yahweh

In other translations that don't use the divine name it is "The Day of the Lord," or sometimes it's called "That Day," because it is the day of days.

We have a vivid account of "That Day" in the second chapter of Isaiah, starting with the tenth verse. I'll read a section of it:

> Get among the rocks,
> hide in the dust,
> at the sight of the terror of Yahweh,

---

[3] [Biblical references are to the Jerusalem Bible, unless otherwise noted as follows: AV, Authorized (King James) Version; NAB, New American Bible; NKJV, New King James Version.—Ed.]

at the brilliance of his majesty,
when he arises to make the earth quake.

Human pride will lower its eyes,
the arrogance of men will be humbled.
Yahweh alone shall be exalted,
on that day.
Yes, that will be the day of Yahweh Sabaoth
against all pride and arrogance,
against all that is great, to bring it down,
against all the cedars of Lebanon
and all the oaks of Bashan,
against all the high mountains
and all the soaring hills,
against all the lofty towers
and all the sheer walls,
against all the ships of Tarshish
and all things of price. . . .

Human pride will be humbled,
the arrogance of men will be brought low.
Yahweh along will be exalted,
on that day,
and all idols thrown down.

Go into the hollows of the rocks,
into the caverns of the earth,
at the sight of the terror of Yahweh,
at the brilliance of his majesty,
when he arises
to make the earth quake.

That day man will fling to moles and bats the idols of silver and the
idols of gold that he made for worship,

and go into the crevices of the rocks
and the rifts of the crag,
at the sight of the terror of Yahweh,
at the brilliance of his majesty,
when he arises
to make the earth quake. (2:10-21)

This image of the Day of Yahweh can be understood psychologically to
refer to an eschatological projection of an anticipated encounter of the ego
with the activated Self. And what is emphasized in the above passage is
how all the inflated tendencies of the ego, any pretensions, anything of

height or elevation or pride, will be destroyed in the process of that encounter. One way I formulate this is that such an encounter dissolves any tendency of the ego to identify with the Self and to take on an authority and value not its own.

That same image, which was lived with for many centuries, has been elaborated in a somewhat different context in the *Dies Irae*, the wrath of God hymn of the Catholic burial mass. It is so vivid in its imagery that I want to read some of it to you. This will give you a real flavor of what the medieval Christian psyche lived with, so far as this particular archetypal image is concerned.

> That day of wrath, that dreadful day
> When heaven and earth shall pass away
> Both David and the Sybil say.
> What terror then to us shall fall
> When lo, the judges steps appall
> About to weigh the deeds of all.
>
> The mighty trumpets' dolorous tones
> Shall pierce through each sepulchral stone,
> And summon men before the throne.
> Now death and nature in amaze
> Behold the Lord his creatures raise
> To meet the judges awful gaze.
> The book is opened that the dead
> May hear their doom from what is read,
> The record of our conscience dread.
> The Lord of Judgment on his throne
> Shall every secret thing make known,
> No sin escapes that once was sown.
>
> Ah, how shall I that day endure,
> What patron's aid can make secure,
> When scarce the just themselves are sure?
> O King of dreadful majesty
> Who grants us grace and mercy free,
> Grant mercy now and grace to me.
> My feeble prayers can make no claim.
> Yet gracious Lord for your great name
> Redeem me from the quenchless flame.
>
> At your right hand give me a place.
> Among your sheep, a child of grace—
> Far from the goat's accursed race.

And when your justly kindled ire
Lets sinners fall to ceaseless fire.
O call me to your chosen choir.
In suppliant prayer I humbly bend
In my contrite heart like ashes rend
Regard, O Lord, my final end.

O on that day, that tearful day
When man to judgement wakes from clay
Do you the sinner's sentence stay
O spare him God we humbly pray.
And grant to all O Savior blest
To die in you the saint's sweet rest.

That hymn emphasizes the judgment aspect of the Day of Yahweh when it says, "What terror then to us shall fall / When lo, the judges' steps appall / About to weigh the deeds of all." This weighing of deeds is a reference to the ancient Egyptian image—I believe they were the originators—of the projection onto the afterlife of a judgment to come. The Egyptian image is that after death the heart of the deceased is weighed on a balance. On one pan is the heart, and on the other is placed a feather which symbolizes Maat, the goddess of truth. If they don't balance out exactly, then that soul is doomed.

The picture on the next page shows the judgment scene. On the left side is a balance, with the jackal-headed god Anubis handling the balance. The heart of the deceased is on one pan and the feather I spoke of is on the other. Thoth, the ibis-headed god, is standing ready to record the findings. This is the "being weighed in the balance" of the last judgment. And right next to Thoth, who is doing the recording, is a very ugly looking monster. It has a crocodile head, a lion's torso and the hind quarters of a hippopotamus. It is called Am-mit. It is the devourer of the unjustified. So if one doesn't make it, doesn't pass this balance test, one's soul is devoured by this monster.

If one does make it, then what's shown on the right side of the picture takes place: the deceased is introduced to the presence of Osiris, which takes place in the hall of the gods. Out of view here Osiris is enthroned. What takes place then is that the soul of the dead man is Osirified, in other words becomes an Osiris, eternal.

This Egyptian symbolism is really an astonishingly explicit description of the ego's encounter with the Self, projected onto the afterlife. To be

The soul of the deceased being weighed in the balance.
(From the papyrus of Ani, British Museum; reproduced in
E.A. Wallis Budge, *The Gods of the Egyptians.*)

devoured by the monster would correspond to succumbing to a psychosis in the encounter with the Self. I've often wondered why the psycho-galvanic phenomenon, the basis of the modern lie detector test, wasn't used by Jung as an example of the workings of the Self. But it is a demon-stration of the fact that the ego cannot get away with dishonesty even physiologically. Our own body will bear witness against us, if we're not loyal to the goddess of truth, an example of the archetypal image of the balance that's pictured here. Something in us won't let us get away with it.

Medieval Christianity picked up this imagery of the soul being weighed in the balance and called it the Last Judgment (opposite). You find such images carved on the cathedrals—sometimes over the entrance ways. And it was associated with the Second Coming of Christ, which is almost a literal transfer of the Egyptian alternatives. The ancient Egyptian alterna-tives were either being judged to be righteous and therefore to become a guest of Osiris, to be accepted by Osiris, or to be eaten by the monster. The medieval Christian view was of the same thing: you either go to heaven and join the enthroned heavenly Christ with the rest of the saints, or you go to hell—the picture of which was very often represented by a devouring monster with great jaws. So it's the same image.

The Archangel Michael weighing souls.
(Van der Weyden, 15th century; Bourgogne, Hospice de Beaume.
Reproduced in S.G.F. Brandon, *The Judgment of the Dead.*)

There's an interesting medieval Jewish description of the theme of the last judgment. What I'm going to quote here derives from an exegetical Midrash on Ecclesiastes that was compiled in the eighth century. I take this particular material from a book called *The Messiah Texts* by Raphael Patai, which I would recommend to you. He's gone to the trouble to bring together just about all the texts, starting with the Bible and the Apocrypha, going through the Talmud and Midrashic texts and the legends—just about everything concerning the descriptions of the anticipated Messiah. Here is one passage, where Rabbi Ruben tells a parable:

> Rabbi Ruben told a parable. The king gave a banquet and invited guests and issued instructions saying, "Everyone should bring along with him that on which he will sit." Some brought rugs and some brought mats and some brought mattresses and some brought covers, and some brought chairs and some brought wood, and some brought stones. The king observed [it] and said, "Everyone should sit on what he brought." Those who sat on the wood and the stones complained against the king and said, "Is this [according to] the honor of the king that we should sit on the wood and the stones?" When the king heard this he said to them, "Is it not enough that you deface the palace with stones and wood which stood in my way in several exits? Must you add insolence and band together to accuse me? It is not I who gives you honor, but you yourselves!"
>
> Thus in the Future to Come the wicked will be sentenced to Gehenna and they will complain against the Holy One, blessed be He: "We were waiting for the salvation of the Holy One, blessed be He, and now is this what happens to us?" The Holy One, blessed be He, says to them: "In the world in which you were, were you not men of quarrels and of evil tongue, and of all kinds of iniquity? Were you not people of strife and violence? . . . Therefore, now walk in the light of your fire and in the sparks which you lit! And say not that this came upon you from My hands; no, but you did it for yourselves. Therefore you will lie down in anguish for it came from your own hands."[4]

This, of course, brings up the very interesting psychological question, "What belongs to the ego and what belongs to the Self?" There's no hard and fast line about that; it's what you might call a floating frontier. Anyhow, that particular text attributes the fire the sinners were consigned to in Gehenna as being brought by themselves.

---

[4] *The Messiah Texts*, pp. 215f.

It's interesting that both this Midrash and the *Dies Irae* emphasize fire as a part of the last judgment. In other words we're dealing with *calcinatio* symbolism.[5] This is made explicit in the 33rd chapter of Isaiah.

> "Now I stand up," says Yahweh
> "now I rise to my full height.
> You have conceived chaff, you will give birth to straw,
> my breath shall devour you like fire.
>
> "The peoples will be reduced to lime,
> like cut thorns they will be burned in the fire.
> You who are far away, listen to what I have done,
> and you who are near, realize my strength."
>
> Sinners in Zion are struck with horror
> and fear seizes on the godless.
> Which of us can live with this devouring fire,
> which of us exist in everlasting flames?
>
> —He who acts with integrity,
> who speaks sincerely
> and rejects extortionate profit,
> who waves away bribes from his hands,
> shuts suggestions of murder out of his ears
> and closes his eyes against crime;
>
> this man will dwell in the heights,
> he will find refuge in a citadel built on rock,
> bread will be given him, he shall not want for water. (33:10-16)

So here the divine manifestation is explicitly described as a fire.

The basic alchemical image pertaining to *calcinatio* is that the *materia* must be subjected to a calcining fire which will then burn away all its dross, all that's impure, all that's corruptible and evanescent. And then what is left finally in the bottom of the retort is described either as white ash or as a vitreous body. They're symbolically equivalent—the ash or the vitreous body. The vitreous or glassy body is one of the possible consequences of the *calcinatio* process. But in either case what's left is then incorruptible. It's eternal; it can no longer be affected by fire even if put to fire again, nothing more can be done to it. So the eternal essence has been produced by means of the calcining fire.

---

[5] [See Edinger, *The Anatomy of the Psyche: Alchemical Symbolism in Psychotherapy,* chap. 2.—Ed.]

The Righteous Remnant

This image of the remaining ash or vitreous body leads directly into the next image I want to discuss from Isaiah, that of the righteous remnant. The righteous remnant Isaiah speaks about is a portion of the people that will survive the Day of Yahweh, survive the encounter with Yahweh's wrath. For instance, on that day,

> Those who are left of Zion
> and remain of Jerusalem
> shall be called holy
> and those left in Jerusalem, noted down for survival. (4:3)

And further on, when that day comes:

> the remnant of Israel and the survivors of the House of Jacob
> will stop relying on the man who strikes them
> and will truly rely on Yahweh,
> the Holy One of Israel.
>
> A remnant will return, the remnant of Jacob,
> to the mighty God. (10:20-21)

Now let me just compare a couple of alchemical statements with those Biblical ones. These are alchemical recipes—descriptions of the alchemical process. Paracelsus says:

> By the element of fire all that is unpurified is destroyed and taken away.
> In the absence of all ordeal by fire there is no proving of a substance possible.
> Fire separates that which is constant or fixed from that which is fugitive or volatile.[6]

Another alchemist, speaking of the stuff in the bottom of his retort that has been subjected to fire, says:

> It is not unfitly compared with Christ, when the putrefied body of the Sun lies dead, inactive, like ashes in the bottom of a phial. . . . So also did it happen to Christ himself, when at the Mount of Olives, and on the cross, he was roasted by the fire of the divine wrath.[7]

We have another image of the righteous remnant in chapter 6, where it is described like the stump of a tree. We read:

---

[6] *The Hermetic and Alchemical Writings of Paracelsus,* 1:4. [See also Edinger, *Anatomy of the Psyche,* p. 32.—Ed.]
[7] Quoted in *Anatomy of the Psyche,* pp. 32f.

There will be a great emptiness in the country
And, though a tenth of the people remain,
it will be stripped like a terebinth [a tree]
of which, once felled, only the stock remains.
The stock is a holy seed. (6:12-13)

This image of a cut-down tree from which a new sprout can grow is also an alchemical image. There is a picture of it on the title page of *Le Songe de Poliphile* (1600)—a great stump with a new sprout growing up from it (next page). It is an image of the process of *mortificatio,* the transformation of libido from one level of manifestation to another.[8] It is a death and rebirth image, and Isaiah uses that very same archetypal image in describing the Day of Yahweh and its consequences: the nation will be stripped like a tree with only a stump remaining. The righteous remnant will be like a new sprout, because the stock is holy seed.

The image of a tree being cut down and new life sprouting up from it also shows up in dreams. It is a basic image referring to the transformation process in which the natural man is transformed into spiritual man or into another level of psychic manifestation through the conscious encounter with the Self.

The Messiah

Let us turn to another image, or another aspect of it, since these all point to the same central meaning, the Messiah. The judging, fiery Day of Yahweh is the threatening, dangerous aspect of the advent of the Messiah. It's part of the same phenomenon, but it's that experience as anticipated by the sinful/fearful ego. Now I want to pay attention to the positive aspect, the illuminating, life-bringing, rescuing and nourishing aspect of the archetypal image of the coming of the Messiah.

There are two major passages in Isaiah that refer to the positive aspect of the coming of the Messiah. The first is in chapter 9 which reads in part:

The people that walked in darkness
has seen a great light;
on those who live in a land of deep shadow
a light has shone.
. . . .
For there is a child born for us,
a son given to us

---

[8] [See Edinger, *Anatomy of the Psyche,* chap. 6.—Ed.]

Representation of the symbolic process, which begins in chaos
and ends with the birth of the phoenix.
(Title page, Béroalde de Verville, *Le Tableau des riches inventions*
or *Le Songe de Poliphile*, 1600; in CW 12, fig. 4.)

and dominion is laid on his shoulders;
and this is the name they give him:
Wonder-Counselor, Mighty-God,
Eternal-Father, Prince-of-Peace.
Wide is his dominion
in a peace that has no end. (9:1, 5-7)

The other text is the magnificent messianic prophecy in chapter 11:

A shoot springs from the stock of Jesse,
[that's the very image I've been talking about; a fresh shoot from a cut
stock]
a scion thrusts from his roots:
on him the spirit of Yahweh rests,
a spirit of wisdom and insight,
a spirit of counsel and power,
a spirit of knowledge and of the fear of Yahweh.
(The fear of Yahweh is his breath.)
He does not judge by appearances,
he gives no verdict on hearsay,
but judges the wretched with integrity,
and with equity gives a verdict for the poor of the land.
His word is a rod that strikes the ruthless,
his sentences bring death to the wicked.

Integrity is the loincloth around his waist,
faithfulness the belt about his hips.

The wolf lives with the lamb,
the panther lies down with the kid,
calf and lion cub feed together
with a little boy to lead them.
The cow and the bear make friends,
their young lie down together.
The lion eats straw like the ox.
The infant plays over the cobra's hole;
into the viper's lair
the young child puts his hand.
They do no hurt, no harm,
on all my holy mountain,
for the country is filled with the knowledge of Yahweh
as the waters swell the sea. (11:1-9)

Much of the legendary material makes clear that the coming of the Messiah brings back the state of paradise. And that's made more or less explicit in this passage where the opposites are reconciled.

What that suggests psychologically is that the unconscious union of opposites—which exists in the original state of the Self, in the unconscious state of the Self, represented by the original Garden of Eden condition—is retrieved on a conscious level with the coming of the Messiah, with the coming of the Self consciously. So that the paradise image, or the Garden of Eden condition, is retrieved consciously to the extent that one has a relation to the Self because that involves a reconciliation of opposites; one is released from the conflict of the opposites. And therefore all the epithets pertaining to peace are part of the phenomenology of the coming of the Messiah.

Now this is a vast and complex symbol, the symbol of the Messiah. I want to just touch a few points about it. In addition to Patai's *Messiah Texts,* I would recommend Gershom Scholem's "The Messianic Idea in Judaism," an essay which gives the title to a book of his. In that essay he brings together many of the legends and speculations about the Messiah as conditions that will pertain. A few of them are particularly relevant psychologically. According to one legend, three things come unawares: the Messiah, a found article and a scorpion.[9] A little ambiguity, you see, about the coming of the Messiah. And that runs through much of the legendary material. It's not all positive, by any means. That corresponds to the fact that the Day of Yahweh and the way it's described, part of the Messianic coming, is not much fun either.

The Talmud quotes the statement by three famous teachers of the third and fourth centuries who say: "May He come, but I don't want to see Him."[10] May he come, but not on my watch, so to speak. According to another legend the Messiah will not come until the tears of Esau have been exhausted.[11] Jacob sinned against Esau, and the idea is that until that basic conflict and wound between Jacob and Esau has been healed, the Self can't come. Another legend says that in the days of the Messiah, man will no longer quarrel with his fellow but with himself.[12] Isn't that remarkable? Another says that when the Messiah comes the day of atonement, the occasion for fasting and self-discipline, will be "like Purim"[13]—which is the

---

[9] Scholem, *The Messianic Idea in Judaism,* p. 11.
[10] Ibid., p. 13.
[11] Ibid., p. 34.
[12] Ibid., p. 35
[13] Ibid., p. 55.

day of joy and feasting. In other words the opposites will be united. Another one: When the Messiah comes the commandments of the Torah will be dissolved, and the Lord will allow the forbidden.[14] Other places say that when the Messiah comes there'll be a new Torah.[15] So the old law will be abrogated and there will be a new law.

The Messianic Banquet

To me one of the most interesting aspects of Messianic symbolism is the image of the Messianic Banquet. We find that described in chapter 25 of Isaiah, which reads:

> On this mountain,
> Yahweh Sabaoth will prepare for all peoples
> a banquet of rich food, a banquet of fine wines,
> of food rich and juicy, of fine strained wines.
> On this mountain he will remove
> the mourning veil covering all peoples,
> and the shroud enwrapping all nations,
> he will destroy Death for ever.
> The Lord Yahweh will wipe away
> the tears from every cheek;
> he will take away his people's shame
> everywhere on earth. (25:6-8)

It's this image of the banquet that I want to concentrate on.

In the Babylonian Talmud, and this I get also from Patai's interesting account of the Messianic Banquet, it says:

> God created a male and a female Leviathan, and had they copulated they . . . would have destroyed the whole world. What did the Holy One, blessed be He, do? He castrated the male and killed the female and preserved her in salt for the pious in the Future to Come. And also . . . Behemoth . . . he created male and female, and had they copulated they would have destroyed the whole world. What did the Holy One, blessed be He, do? He castrated the male and cooled the female and preserved her for the pious in the Future to Come.[16]

So we have a salted Leviathan and a frozen Behemoth. Now I read on:

---

[14] Ibid.

[15] Ibid.

[16] *The Messiah Texts*, pp. 236f.

> The Holy One, blessed be He, will in the future prepare a banquet for the
> pious from the meat of Leviathan. . . . And they will divide leftovers and
> make of them merchandise in the marketplace of Jerusalem.[17]

You see, what they're going to do with the salted Leviathan and the frozen
Behemoth is provide food for the Messianic Banquet. Now that strikes me
as a very significant symbolic image: the meat of Leviathan and Behemoth
is the food of the Messianic Banquet.

I think what that means, psychologically, is that the eating, the assimi-
lation of primitive desirousness, is what brings the Messiah. In other
words, to the extent one is able to eat the flesh of Leviathan, one thereby
transforms the nature of the Self from its primitive form to its divine form.
We know from the Book of Job that Leviathan and Behemoth are aspects
of the divine nature. If circumstances are such that in the Messianic age
individuals are able to feed off Leviathan, then their very feeding and assimilating of the Leviathan flesh serves the purpose of transforming the
nature of the deity.

I don't think the significance of that image can be underestimated. It is
one example of what I would call the banquet archetype, and it's important because it comes up in dreams. Other major examples of the banquet
archetype are: 1) the 23rd psalm, in which, you remember, Yahweh will
prepare a table for me before my enemies, a banquet; 2) the Platonic dialogue titled "The Banquet" (often translated "The Symposium," but it
means banquet), where the divine nature of eros is the subject matter; 3)
the parable that Christ uses in the 22nd chapter of Matthew in speaking of
the kingdom of heaven as like a wedding banquet; and 4) the Last Supper
and the Eucharistic banquet of Holy Communion, which has grown out of
that image of the last supper.

Those are various amplifications of the banquet archetype that should
be available to you for amplifying dreams, because the image expresses
the nourishing aspect of the Self, the constellation of the Self in its benign,
nourishing, refreshing aspect. Healing and redemption are being offered
via the gift of a banquet from the unconscious.

I want to conclude these remarks with a modern dream of the Messiah
image. This also comes from Patai, and it concerns Theodor Herzl, the
founding father of political Zionism and the father of the modern state of

---

[17] Ibid., p. 237.

Israel. Patai tells us that Herzl grew up in Budapest in an assimilated Jewish family. The Jewish education he received was rudimentary. However, he did have a Bar Mitzvah. And one of the presents he received on the occasion of his Bar Mitzvah, at the age of thirteen, was a book of Jewish legends. In it he read about the coming of the Messiah, whose arrival is awaited daily by many Jews. And many years later he described the reaction he had to reading about that, for it really had captured his imagination. He says, "In the depth of my soul it seems that the legend continued to expand, though I was unaware of it. One night I had a dream."

He doesn't say how long after his Bar Mitzvah he had this dream, but I think it's safe to say he had it at adolescence, probably not too long after his Bar Mitzvah and after he had read that book. Here is his dream:

> King Messiah came, and he was old and glorious. He lifted me in his arms, and he soared with me on the wings of the wind. On one of the clouds, full of splendor, we met the figure of Moses (his appearance was like that of Moses hewn in marble by Michelangelo; from my early childhood I liked to look at the photographs of that statue), and the Messiah called to Moses, "For this child I have prayed." Then he turned to me, "Go and announce to the Jews that I will soon come and perform great miracles for my people and for the whole world." I woke up and it was a dream. I kept this dream a secret and did not dare to tell it to anybody.[18]

I think that's quite remarkable in view of what he did accomplish.

---

[18] *The Messiah Texts*, pp. 272f.

2
Isaiah, Part Two

As I mentioned last time, the Book of Isaiah has been split into two or more parts. Chapters 40-66 are thought to have been written by a second Isaiah, coming two hundred years after the first—during the time of the Babylonian exile. The connection between the two is quite justified psychologically and symbolically; since some of the basic images are the same in the two sections. And it really is an organic whole, considered psychologically, for the first part of Isaiah is a book of doom in which the major image, as we talked about last time, is the day of Yahweh's wrath, and the second part of Isaiah is a book of consolation.

Cyclic Encounters with the Self

In the first part of Isaiah the nation is brash and arrogant, largely ignoring Yahweh, and Isaiah is therefore obliged to emphasize that punishment and a state of alienation from Yahweh is going to take place. In the second part of the book the nation is in exile and slavery. True to the compensatory function of the unconscious and of spokesmen for the unconscious, the prophet now speaks of reconnection with Yahweh and of his love, support and eternal concern for Israel. These are the two sides of the ego's cyclic relation to the Self (pictured opposite), and the Book of Isaiah, taken as a whole, reveals that cycle very clearly.

The developmental process really does go through a cycle, again and again and again. Starting with a state of unconscious connection, indeed unconscious identity with the Self, there is a sense of smugness, followed by inflation which when acted upon has the consequence of rejection. The ego experiences rejection, leading to a state of alienation and despair; and then if the process does not get short-circuited but keeps following its organic pathway, that leads to a change of attitude, to a repentance, to a *metanoia*. And with that change of attitude a reconnection with the Self takes place.

Another way of saying it is that each cycle involves a *nekyia*, a descent into the unconscious, a *mortificatio,* a state of *nigredo,* which in turn leads to an encounter with the benevolent, life-sustaining aspects of the Self.

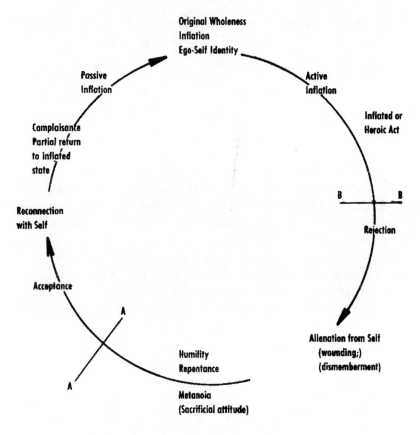

The psychic life cycle.
(From Edinger, *Ego and Archetype*, fig. 5.)

Let me give you some examples. In chapter 59, Yahweh speaks directly to the alienated ego represented by Israel:

> No, the hand of Yahweh is not too short to save,
> nor his ear too dull to hear.
> But iniquities have made a gulf
> between you and your God.
> Your sins have made him veil his face
> so as not to hear you. (59:1-2)

That's the Self speaking to the alienated ego halfway through the cycle. It is put even more forcefully in the Living Bible translation:

> Listen now. The Lord isn't too weak to save you. And he isn't getting deaf! He can hear when you call! But the trouble is your sins have cut you off from God. Because of sin he has turned his face away from you and will not listen anymore.

That describes about as vividly as possible the state of alienation between the ego and the Self.

But that all changes as soon as the ego recognizes its sin—or its mistake, if you will. Or its inflation, its misjudgment, its hubris. Then follows a change of mind, a *metanoia,* which is followed by a change of attitude on the part of the Self. And with that change of attitude, one sees positive Self images as opposed to negative Self images. The general rule is that whenever one has dreams of threatening figures it is an indication that the ego has an improper attitude toward the unconscious. And when that attitude changes, the threat immediately ameliorates and becomes sometimes overtly positive. That's precisely what happens in the Book of Isaiah. And the second part of Isaiah is very largely descriptive of the encounter with the positive Self.

An example of that is found at the beginning of chapter 40:

> A voice cries, "Prepare in the wilderness
> a way for Yahweh.
> Make a straight highway for our God
> across the desert.
> Let every valley be filled in,
> every mountain and hill be laid low,
> let every cliff become a plain,
> and the ridges a valley;
>
> then the glory of Yahweh shall be revealed

> and all mankind shall see it;
> for the mouth of Yahweh has spoken." (40:3-5)

I see this as an especially beautiful example of an image of the emerging ego-Self axis. That is how I understand the expression "highway for our God."

The diagrams below show different stages of relation between the ego and the Self.[19] At the beginning the latent ego is completely contained in the Self. It doesn't exist as a separate being. In the second stage the ego has been partially born out of its identity with the Self, but the connecting link between the two is still unconscious. With further experiences, and further reductive analysis which brings about progressive resolution of ego-Self identity, a greater degree of the ego becomes conscious and separated from the Self. In time it reaches a point where the connecting link between the two becomes conscious. This is the situation I see pictured here in this passage in Isaiah, where a "highway for our God" is referred to. At that point consciousness of a pathway, a connecting link between the ego and the Self, comes into view, and the glory of Yahweh emerges.

I would also like to emphasize the enantiodromia[20] symbolism in that

Stages of ego development

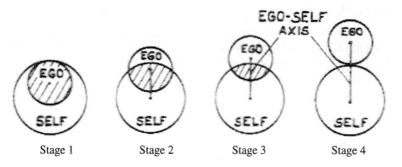

| Stage 1 | Stage 2 | Stage 3 | Stage 4 |

---

[19] [Reproduced from Edinger, *Ego and Archetype*, p. 5. Stage 4, representing the total separation of ego and Self and a complete consciousness of the ego-Self axis, is theoretically possible but probably does not exist in reality.—Ed.]

[20] [Enantiodromia refers to the phenomenon that everything, in the fullness of time, will eventually turn into its opposite. Jung: "The symbolic process . . . usually shows an enantiodromian structure . . . and so represents a rhythm of negative and positive, loss and gain, dark and light." ("Archetypes of the Collective Unconscious," *The Archetypes and the Collective Unconscious,* CW 9i, par. 82)—Ed.]

passage: every high point is going to be made low and every low point is going to be filled up, leveled off. This is characteristic phenomenology of the Self which unites the opposites. As an example, an alchemical text has the Philosophers' Stone saying this about itself:

> I am the mediatrix of the elements, making one to agree with another; that which is warm I make cold, that which is dry I make moist . . . that which is hard I soften, and the reverse.[21]

It is the same idea as lowering what is high and raising up what is low.

The passage about preparing a highway for the Lord also comes up in the descriptions of John the Baptist in the New Testament. All four of the gospels equate John the Baptist with the voice crying in the wilderness that Isaiah speaks of. And Isaiah is quoted explicitly at this point, preparing a way for the Lord, making His path straight. And the task that he performed specifically involved a call for repentance, a baptism for the repentance and forgiveness of sins. This states quite explicitly then that repentance or change of attitude is what opens up a highway to the experience of the Self. And in second Isaiah what comes over that highway are various, profound and beautiful examples of the positive Self: comfort, love and redemption.

I'm going to quote a few of those examples. In chapter 41 Yahweh is talking; He's coming on this highway that's prepared for Him:

> You whom I brought from the confines of the earth
> and called from the ends of the world;
> you to whom I said, "You are my servant,
> I have chosen you, not rejected you,"
>
> do not be afraid, for I am with you;
> stop being anxious and watchful, for I am your God.
> I give you strength, I bring you help,
> I uphold you with my victorious right hand.
> Yes, all those who raged against you,
> shall be put to shame and confusion;
> they who fought against you
> shall be destroyed, and perish.
>
> You will seek but never find them,
> those enemies of yours.

---

[21] Quoted in *Mysterium Coniunctionis*, CW 14, par. 9, n. 42. (CW refers throughout to *The Collected Works of C.G. Jung*)

. . . .

For I, Yahweh, your God,
I am holding you by the right hand;
I tell you, "Do not be afraid,
I will help you."

Do not be afraid, Jacob, poor worm,
Israel, puny mite.
I will help you—it is Yahweh who speaks—
the Holy One of Israel is your redeemer. (41:9-14)

This is the kind of supportive manifestation of the Self that starts to appear at the low point, you see, when things are at their worst. Another example:

The poor and needy ask for water, and there is none,
their tongue is parched with thirst.
I, Yahweh, will answer them,
I, the God of Israel, will not abandon them.

I will make rivers well up on barren heights,
and fountains in the midst of valleys;
turn the wilderness into a lake,
and dry ground into waterspring.

In the wilderness I will put cedar trees,
acacias, myrtles, olives.
In the desert I will plant juniper,
plane tree and cypress side by side;

so that men may see and know,
may all observe and understand
the hand of Yahweh has done this,
that the Holy One of Israel has created it. (41:17-20)

We then have various images of Yahweh as a nourishing mother:

For Zion was saying, "Yahweh has abandoned me,
the Lord has forgotten me."
Does a woman forget her baby at the breast,
or fail to cherish the son of her womb?
Yet even if these forget,
I will never forget you. (49:14-15)

And in chapter 54 there's the promise of eternal love:

Yes, like a forsaken wife, distressed in spirit,
Yahweh calls you back.

Does a man cast off the wife of his youth?
says your God.

I did forsake you for a brief moment,
but with great love will I take you back.
In excess of anger, for a moment
I hid my face from you.
But with everlasting love I have taken pity on you,
says Yahweh, your redeemer.

I am now as I was in the days of Noah
when I swore that Noah's waters
should never flood the world again.
So now I swear concerning my anger with you
and the threats I made against you;

for the mountains may depart,
the hills be shaken,
but my love for you will never leave you
and my covenant of peace with you will never be shaken,
says Yahweh who takes pity on you. (54:6-10)

That is very interesting. It states explicitly that this occasion is a second version of the promise after Noah's flood. You remember at that time the rainbow was set in the sky as the sign of Yahweh's covenant with man that he would never again destroy them by water. And now after a second version of the flood, after the rejection of Israel, the destruction of their land, their exile and deportation, he promises that will never happen again. He promises eternal love.

I think what that means psychologically is that whenever one has had an experience of the unconscious from a sufficient depth, it crystalizes the Self; it constellates this "highway of the Lord," so to speak. That then establishes a solid, reliable foundation for the psyche, so that it is no longer subject to grave invasions by the unconscious. It's as though an analytic process can be a kind of controlled experience of the unconscious which functions as a sort of immunization that protects one from a more dangerous interaction. And following the flood that does not destroy completely comes a promise that it won't happen again.

There are several other items I want to draw your attention to. In chapter 43 we read:

I, I am Yahweh,
there is no other savior but me.

It is I who have spoken, have saved, have made the proclamation,
. . . .
You are my witnesses—it is Yahweh who speaks—
and I, I am your God. (43:11-12)

This makes the very interesting psychological statement that the ego is the witness of the Self. The Greek word for witness is *martyr*, and that's what the early Christian martyrs thought of themselves as being: witnesses for their conviction of Christ as a redeemer, or you might say they bore witness to the reality of Christ. So that's the only way psychic reality can be demonstrated, really—by individuals who bear witness to its reality in they way they live their life. That's the way psychic reality manifests itself externally. The Self becomes visible, so to speak, in the outer world only through certain individual egos that bear witness to it by the way they live. And this passage is a statement of that fact.

In another passage, we read:

And now I have put you in the fire like silver,
I have tested you in the furnace of distress.
For my sake and my sake only have I acted—
is my name to be profaned?
Never will I yield my glory to another. (48:10-11)

Here we have an explicit statement to the effect that the suffering ordeal that man is subjected to is for the sake of the Self: "For my sake and my sake only have I acted." In other words, the ego must endure the suffering that brings greater consciousness, not for the sake of the ego but for the sake of the Self. Because that process is what brings about the transformation of the Self. So the increasing consciousness of the ego is accompanied simultaneously by the transformation the Self for whose sake the ordeal exists.

That same idea is expressed another way in chapter 61, which speaks about the spirit of Yahweh that through his prophet will

. . . comfort all those who mourn and . . . give to them
for ashes a garland;
for mourning robe the oil of gladness,
for despondency, praise.
They are to be called "terebinths of integrity,"
planted by Yahweh to glorify him. (61:2-3)

So, after all evidences of despair, defeat and grief, ashes and mourning, comes victory and praise and the planting of trees of integrity, all for the purpose of glorifying Yahweh. After *mortificatio* comes the appearance of the positive Self.

The Suffering Servant of Yahweh

I want to spend the rest of my remarks on the major image in the second part of Isaiah, this remarkable and enigmatic figure called the Suffering Servant of Yahweh. What's so striking about this figure and his description is that there really is no satisfactory or adequate parallel to this image anywhere else. I bring in some little piddling parallels, but it is notable in its uniqueness. And the Christian myth was really built on this. In fact Christ almost wouldn't have to exist; he could be dreamed up just out of these songs of the Suffering Servant of Yahweh in the second part of Isaiah, plus Psalm 22. If you take Psalm 22, that Messianic Psalm, plus the four passages in chapters 42, 49, 50 and then the one in chapter 52 running over into chapter 53—take those five things and you have the whole Christian myth in a nutshell.

In a footnote in the Jerusalem Bible,[22] a lot is compressed into a small amount that summarizes the material. Here is part of that:

> The four "songs of the servant of Yahweh" present a mysterious "servant" who is in some ways like the servant-Israel of the other passages. And one passage actually identifies him with Israel. But in others, however, he is distinguished from the servant-Israel and contrasted with him by other qualities which show that this mysterious servant is a particular individual. He is called by Yahweh while still in his mother's womb, filled with his spirit; the servant is a "disciple," and Yahweh has opened his ears so that, by establishing justice on earth, he may instruct mankind, sort them and judge them by his word. He performs his task gently and without display. He even appears to fail in it. He accepts outrage and contempt. He does not succumb because Yahweh sustains him. Like Job he is innocent but he is treated as an evil doer whom God has punished, condemned to a shameful death. In fact, however, all this is his own free offering for sinners whose guilt he takes on himself and for whom he intercede. And by a hitherto un-dreamed-of act of power, from this atoning suffering Yahweh brings the salvation of all men. Therefore the servant will grow great. He will "see a posterity" and hordes of the redeemed will be his. He will not only "gather" Israel, but he will be the light of the nations.

---

[22] *Jerusalem Bible,* p. 1209, note *a* to chap. 42 (slightly modified).

It's a very profound and complex symbolic image.

In chapter 42 we read:

> I, Yahweh, have called you to serve the cause of right;
> [he's talking to the Suffering Servant]
> I have taken you by the hand and formed you;
> I have appointed you as a covenant of the people and light of the nations,
>
> to open the eyes of the blind,
> to free captives from prison,
> and those who live in darkness from the dungeon. (42:6-7)

Now we must ask ourselves right at the outset, before going any further, how are we to understand this figure psychologically? I suggest you all consider that. The best formulation I've come up with so far is that the Suffering Servant of Yahweh is a personification of redeeming consciousness. Certainly in this passage, consciousness is emphasized: "open the eyes of the blind" and bring light to those captive in dark prisons.

Another aspect of Yahweh's Suffering Servant is his conscious acceptance of suffering and his willingness to carry the appearance of evil. Here's the fourth song of the Servant of Yahweh, which runs from chapter 52:13 to chapter 53:12. It's quite astonishing.

> See, my servant will prosper,
> he shall be lifted up, exalted, rise to great heights.
>
> As the crowds were appalled on seeing him
> —so disfigured did he look
> that he seemed no longer human—
> so will the crowd be astonished at him,
> and kings stand speechless before him;
> for they shall see something never told
> and witness something never heard before:
> "Who could believe what we have heard,
> and to whom has the power of Yahweh been revealed?"
> Like a sapling he grew up in front of us,
> like a root in arid ground.
> Without beauty, without majesty (we saw him),
> no looks to attract our eyes;
> a thing despised and rejected by men,
> a man of sorrows and familiar with suffering,
> a man to make people screen their faces;
> he was despised and we took no account of him.
>
> And yet ours were the sufferings he bore,

ours the sorrows he carried.
But we, we thought of him as someone punished,
struck by God, and brought low.
Yet was pierced through for our faults,
crushed for our sins.
On him lies a punishment that brings us peace,
and through his wounds we are healed.

We had all gone astray like sheep,
each taking his own way,
and Yahweh burdened him
with the sins of all of us.
Harshly dealt with, he bore it humbly,
he never opened his mouth,
like a lamb that is led to the slaughterhouse,
like a sheep that is dumb before its shearers
never opening its mouth.

By force and by law he was taken;
would anyone plead his cause?
Yes, he was torn away from the land of the living;
for our faults struck down in death.
They gave him a grave with the wicked,
a tomb with the rich,
though he had done no wrong
and there had been no perjury in his mouth.
. . . .

By his sufferings shall my servant justify many,
taking their faults on himself.

Hence I will grant whole hordes for his tribute,
he shall divide the spoil with the mighty,
for surrendering himself to death
and letting himself be taken for a sinner,
while he was bearing the faults of many
and praying all the time for sinners.

Now how are we to understand that?

The best parallels—the only ones I've been able to come up with for
this image—are the scapegoat ritual that we learn about in Leviticus, and
the *pharmakos* ritual in ancient Greece.[23] You remember in Leviticus we

---

[23] [See Edinger, *The Bible and the Psyche*, pp. 155f., and Walter Burkert, *Greek Religion*, pp. 82ff.—Ed.]

were told about the scapegoat ritual in which the sins of Israel were heaped on a goat which was then led out into the wilderness. (Lev. 16:20-22) And the idea was that all the evil that had accumulated would be removed, banished, with the goat.

Something very similar to that took place in ancient Athens: what was called the *pharmakos* ritual. This would be a ritual purification of the city that would be done especially in times of trouble or pestilence. At one time some derelict or criminal would be used. He would be ritually heaped with all the evil that existed in the city. He would be beaten and then led out of the city—either killed or banished. By that device then, by having all the guilt and evil of the city put on him, the city would be cleansed. And by the stripes of his beating the city would be purified. The word for such a person was the word *pharmakos*, which is a masculine form. The neuter form of the same word is *pharmakon*—which means a medicine or a drug. So you see how closely interconnected are the two ideas of the purifying scapegoat and the healing medicine. ·

Now that certainly is a partial parallel, at least, to the way the Suffering Servant of Yahweh is described. Except you might say he was both a *pharmakos* and a *pharmakon*. And the unique feature of the Suffering Servant Yahweh is that it was a willing sacrifice. He was conscious. So I see this figure as an image of redeeming consciousness. A consciousness that is in contact with the Self, with wholeness, and can bear an unusual degree of awareness of evil without personal despair. If one is aware that the evil being attached to one is archetypal, collective evil, and doesn't identify with it personally, that makes it more bearable. The great danger in experiencing oneself as evil is that it can lead to total demoralization, despair and a state of impotent unworthiness.

What this image and description bring to mind is the whole problem of being able to endure consciousness of evil—not consciousness of evil outside, but consciousness of evil inside. That in part is what makes the experience of wholeness so rare and difficult to endure, because it includes the experience of being evil. Evil is a substantial reality; that is certainly evidenced by the scapegoat or the *pharmakos* ritual. Early man experienced it as a profound and urgent reality. And if you have eyes to see you can see it all around you: human beings have almost no capacity to endure awareness of their own evil. Just a wee little glimpse of the evil aspect of oneself and one is overwhelmed and demoralized.

This means then that continued human existence demands that containers be found for evil. And this, of course, accounts for the universality of shadow projections. As long as evil can be located out there in the criminal element, or whatever other category one uses as the container of evil, then one's self-esteem is at least sufficient to carry on. That's always the issue. Self-esteem is fragile, and awareness of too much evil can just overwhelm it.

But what we learn from these passages of the Suffering Servant of Yahweh is that there is an agency able to endure evil. And it has redemptive power. I see that agency as consciousness—consciousness that is aware of the transpersonal dimension of the psyche and therefore does not make the fatal mistake of identifying with everything it discovers within. This is the point Jung made so much of. Once you start seeing what is really there, you had better not identify with it; otherwise you are a gonner. And that's the phenomenon that I see the Suffering Servant of Yahweh referring to.

You might say, then, that to the extent the Suffering Servant figure is visible, one is thereby released or redeemed both from the projection of evil and identification with evil. This means that there's a certain immunity, a certain safety, on the one hand, that does not require that one project the evil into others. It also means that if one is the recipient of a projection of evil, of the shadow, one doesn't identify with the projection, which is not so easy to avoid—since it's an unconscious process, one often doesn't know what's happening. I think the phenomenology of the Suffering Servant of Yahweh redeems one from those dangerous aspects of encounters with evil.

Now, as perhaps you know, Jung was very closely related to the image of the Suffering Servant of Yahweh. The reason I know this is that he used a Suffering Servant passage as the opening epigraph for his book *Psychology and Alchemy*. The passage he used was this: "The bruised reed he shall not break, and the smoking flax he shall not quench. . . ." To put that in its larger context, the whole passage reads as follows:

> Here is my servant whom I uphold,
> my chosen one in whom my soul delights.
> I have endowed him with my spirit
> that he may bring true justice to the nations.
>
> He does not cry out or shout aloud,

or make his voice heard in the streets.
He does not break the crushed reed,
nor quench the wavering flame. (42:1-3)

I think the most immediate reason for that motto was Jung's concern to write in a way that would do no psychological damage to anybody. He was in a quandary as to how to present his psychological findings which pertain to the religious images of the psyche, how to present the empirical approach to those images, without damaging anyone's traditional, religious or creedal relation to the same figures. That is quite a ticklish business. Jung was very sensitive to that problem. It's practically insoluble because you have to talk out of both sides of your mouth at the same time. He does that in places. And the explanation is given in this motto: he doesn't want to break the bruised reeds nor quench the smoldering wicks, so he didn't want to put out the weak and dimly lighted consciousnesses. And that's one of the aspects of the Suffering Servant. Jung was aware of the potentially negative and destructive shadow side of what he had to say for some people; therefore he did his best to present it in a way that would do no damage.

Finally, in connection with this image of the Suffering Servant, I want to quote a portion of a famous letter in which Jung says,

> I consciously and intentionally made my life miserable because I wanted God to be alive and free from the suffering man has put on him by loving his own reason more than God's secret intentions.[24]

I think we could say that that remark comes from the archetype of the Suffering Servant of Yahweh. One might ask: isn't it perverse or masochistic to go in search of suffering? Well, not if one knows what one's doing. I think that whenever we glimpse a painful complex or problem, we have to make a choice. We have to choose whether to try to avoid it or whether we're going to go toward it and meet it squarely. What Jung is saying here is that he pursued and embraced his sufferings as he found them in order to relieve the unconscious of that burden. That then allows the unconscious to function naturally. And this is what we do when we deliberately explore the unconscious and bring painful problems into consciousness. It releases the growth capacity of the unconscious. It also helps

---

[24] See Gerhard Adler, "Aspects of Jung's Personality and Work," in *Psychological Perspectives*, vol. 6, no. 1 (Spring 1975), p. 12.

to save ourselves and our external environment from the evil consequences of projections.

There is another aspect to this, which has to do with the dynamic between the opposites. The psyche cannot be precisely delimited; the personal psyche merges into the collective psyche without a clear boundary. The psyche operates on the basis of opposites and the compensatory interplay between them. This means that if one experiences a particularly extreme, one-sided state, it must necessarily constellate its contrary. That is the way the psyche operates. It often happens on an unconscious level, of course; we can be tossed back and forth between extremes unconsciously. But if one consciously chooses one extreme, its opposite is automatically constellated.

That psychological fact is one of the aspects of the Suffering Servant of Yahweh—and it also underlies the symbolism of the myth of Christ where the extreme of suffering and death is consciously chosen. The consequence of that is the manifestation of its opposite: eternal glory. There's a psychological reality in the dynamic between those opposites, and the Suffering Servant image alludes to it.

This is a mysterious business, but it's a reality.

3
Jeremiah, Part One

In the first half of Jeremiah we make the acquaintance of perhaps the supreme Old Testament prophet, the outstanding, fullest example of what an Old Testament prophet is. Jeremiah is really a kind of paradigm of the archetype of the prophet, making that image extraordinarily clear.

The Prophet Archetype

I thought we might spend a few minutes just considering the implications of the image of the prophet as an archetype. The etymology of the word comes from two roots: *pro,* meaning before, in front of, and *phátis,* meaning voice or oracle, so it means "to speak out before all." That's the Greek derivation. Another word for prophet in Greek is the word *mántis,* from which we get our term "mantic." *Mántis* means a diviner or seer, so the word *mánteuma* means an oracle. A verb is derived from that, *manteúomai,* which means to deliver an oracle—in effect, to prophesy.

Likewise there are two major Hebrew words that are used for prophet, actually three, but two chief ones. The word *nabi,* which is always translated prophet; then the word *ro'eh* which is the active participle of the verb to see, and therefore is translated as seer, the seeing one. And then there is another word, *hozeh,* that also derives from a verb, to see. But the word *nabi,* which is translated as prophet, derives from an Akkadian root referring to one who calls or who is called.

That gives us three variants of the archetypal image of the prophet. He is the one who speaks before others. And what does he speak? He speaks what he sees; he has to be a seer in order to speak. And where does the urge or the assignment to speak come from? It comes from being called to do so. I think those three aspects of the etymology are all relevant to the archetypal image.

Psychologically the prophet would refer to one who sees the transpersonal reality and therefore can be an oracle by revealing that reality. And also the prophet is one who is called to transmit or communicate to the everyday personal world what he sees of the transpersonal or archetypal dimension. He or she is called to speak forth the vision and also to be a caller to others, in addition to being a called one.

I think this is a very important dynamic image psychologically which works below the surface in a great many ways in the motivation of individuals. One might distinguish two aspects of the manifestation of the prophet archetype: the extraverted and the introverted aspect.

The extraverted aspect, which is the visible one so far as the literal lives of the prophets are concerned, refers to an individual who serves a mediating function between the inner world of awareness and the outer world. Examples would be artists, for instance, who are seers, have an inner vision, but are then called to mediate that inner vision by means of their creations. And in the process they may be called to alter the *Zeitgeist*. I think authentic political activists—not the neurotic political activist, the ones who project inner issues onto the political arena, but those who are really destined to be authentic activists, who are called to alter the collective attitude and the outer state of things—are also examples of the extraverted aspect of the prophet archetype.

The other aspect, the introverted aspect, would be something that takes place within the individual psyche. In that case the figure of the prophet would mediate messages between the ego and the unconscious. We might think of this aspect of the prophet, then, as the personification of the transcendent function. So one would consult the prophet in active imagination, for instance. And I believe it's this introverted aspect of the prophet archetype that is often projected onto the analyst or activated in the analytic process and carried initially by the analyst, temporarily, until the patient is ready to take it over and recognize it as an inner function of his or her own psyche. Those are some thoughts I have about the implications of the prophet image as an archetype.

But now let's consider some of the aspects of prophethood in the case of Jeremiah, as we discover it in his book.

The Prophethood of Jeremiah

We're told right at the very beginning of the first chapter that Jeremiah was destined from the womb for his prophetic function. Yahweh says:

> Before I formed you in the womb I knew you;
> before you came to birth I consecrated you;
> I have appointed you as a prophet to the nations. (1:5)

This reminds me of an alchemical parallel, a text that says, speaking about being called to be an alchemist:

> There are but a few stocks that are fitted to innoculate the grafts of this science on [this science meaning alchemy]; they are mysteries incommunicable to any but the adepts and those that have been devoted even from their cradles to serve and wait at this altar.[25]

Here the same idea is presented that certain individuals were chosen in their cradles, so to speak, to become alchemists. I think what's meant here psychologically is that the potential for a reasonably high level of individuation is innate. It's built in; it's not determined by environment or conditioning; it's built into one from the beginning. It has a predetermined aspect, and as a result it almost invariably manifests itself in some form in childhood. I think the most common manifestation is that the child experiences rather powerful feelings of separateness and painful alienation from the collective. That is almost always the case of individuals who later are destined for a considerable degree of individuation. And we have in these passages, also, the idea of being singled out, called, elected, of being chosen in a kind of innate way. And this is an authentic psychological fact, that certain people are set apart just by their very nature. Nature is aristocratic in this sense, and creates an authentic psychological elite, which is very different from any presumptuous or inflated notions of superiority. Yahweh is telling Jeremiah, really, that he is such person, and that he was established as such from conception.

In this same first chapter Jeremiah responds to his call in a characteristic way. He protests, saying he can't be a prophet, he doesn't know how to speak, he's just a child (1:6). And Yahweh then touches his mouth, indicating that he will put the words into his mouth.

Now over and beyond the regressive aspect of this protestation I think there is another idea expressed here when Jeremiah says he's a child. I think we might see it as referring to the fact that the call, and the content of the call, comes via the child side of the psyche—in other words via the less developed, inferior, undifferentiated aspect of the psyche. And that's one reason why it is resisted and feared—because it exposes the recipient to his or her own weakest and most childlike side.

In any case Jeremiah's protest is ineffective, and he is then commanded to look. Yahweh says, "'Jeremiah, what do you see?'" (1:11) And Jere-

---

[25] [Source unknown.—Ed.]

miah looks and he sees a branch of the almond tree called the Watchful Tree; and on a second occasion he sees a boiling cooking pot that's tilting from the north. Yahweh then interprets these images: "I too watch over my word to see it fulfilled," and "The North is where disaster is boiling over." (1:12, 14)

I think we can extract something else from these images too, but first of all it would be significant that Jeremiah is commanded to look. I take that to be an order to do active imagination: "Look, what image do you see?" First comes the image and then comes the question, "What does the image mean?" Yahweh is the one that supplies the meaning in this case. Jeremiah supplies the image: he looks and sees, and then Yahweh tells him what it means. And these two images then turn out to be part of the message that Jeremiah is supposed to announce, as Yahweh interprets them. If a patient brought these images to me I would interpret them a little differently. I would interpret them as meaning that Jeremiah is being shown by these images two of the basic aspects of the individuation process: watching and cooking. Seeing and being seen on the one hand, and being cooked and being the cooker on the other hand. Those are the most basic implications of the two images.

Anyway, Jeremiah is obliged then to do something with these images. First he is directed to look at them, to look and see what they are; then he is told what they mean, but that doesn't finish it, because finally he is obliged to do something. This corresponds to Jung's statement that images must be integrated psychologically and their ethical consequences extracted. I want to read you a statement of Jung's about this matter, because I think it is very important that one not just confine oneself to looking:

> My science was the only way I had of extricating myself from that chaos. Otherwise the material would have trapped me in its thicket, strangled me like jungle creepers. I took great care to try to understand every single image [he was looking, you see, just as Jeremiah was told to do], every item of my psychic inventory, and to classify them scientifically—so far as this was possible—and, above all, to realize them in actual life. That is what we usually neglect to do. We allow the images to rise up, and maybe we wonder about them, but that is all. We do not take the trouble to understand them, let alone draw ethical conclusions from them. This stopping-short conjures up the negative effects of the unconscious.
>
> It is equally a grave mistake to think it is enough to gain some understanding of the images and that knowledge can here make a halt. Insight into

them must be converted into ethical obligation. Not to do so is to fall pray to the power principle, and this produces dangerous effects which are destructive, not only to others, but even to the knower. The images of the unconscious place a great responsibility upon man. Failure to understand them or shirking of ethical responsibility deprives him of his wholeness and imposes a painful fragmentariness on his life.[26]

The ethical responsibility that was imposed on Jeremiah was to communicate to his people the messages he had received. As we'll see, that was an exceedingly heavy burden that he bore only with the greatest reluctance.

The interesting feature of Jeremiah, I think more so than any other prophet, is the number of episodes where he is required to act out certain images in his own life. One of those examples is the loincloth episode in chapter 13, which reads as follows:

Yahweh said this to me, "Go and buy a linen loincloth and put it around your waist. But do not dip it in water." And so . . . I bought a loincloth and put it around my waist. A second time the word of Yahweh was spoken to me, "Take the loincloth that you have bought and are wearing around your waist; up! Go to the Euphrates and hide it in a hole in the rock." [Which he did.]. . . . Many days afterward Yahweh said to me, "Get up and go to the Euphrates and fetch the loincloth . . . ." [So I went and] took the loincloth from the place where I had hidden it. . . . [Now it] was spoiled, good for nothing [because it was rotten by then, mildewed]. Then the word of Yahweh was addressed to me, "Thus says Yahweh: In the same way I will spoil the arrogance of Judah and Jerusalem. This evil people who refuse to listen to my words, who follow the dictates of their own hard hearts, who have followed alien gods, and served them and worshipped them, let them become like this loincloth, good for nothing. For just as a loincloth clings to a man's waist, so I had intended the whole House of Judah to cling to me . . . to be my people, my glory, my honour and my boast. But they have not listened." (13:1-11)

I think there's a very significant psychological fact expressed in such images as this: emerging images from the unconscious may often manifest themselves first in the individual's lived reality. He finds himself—either by his own inner urge and inclination or as a result of some circumstance that comes to him from without—living out a situation that has as its root the symbolic image that he needs to understand.

---

[26] *Memories, Dreams, Reflections,* p. 192.

Ralph Waldo Emerson, with that incredible insight I can scarcely believe he could possess, was aware of this phenomenon. He describes it in a couple of sentences—kind of a hard nut to crack, you have to read them twice to get it:

> Every man's condition is a solution in hieroglyphic to those inquiries he would put. He acts it as life, before he apprehend it as truth."[27]

This is a subtle idea, but one place to look for the relevant symbolic images that are emerging from the unconscious is just to look at the way you are living life, what you are doing, and what your inclinations lead you to actually perform. And you may discover that you are doing something like burying loincloths, as Jeremiah did.

I'm going to give you a personal example of such a thing. Some of you may have heard this. It is what I call my tree story. Many years ago I decided that my front yard needed some trees on it, some evergreen trees. So I went to a place where they had a lot of evergreens. They were growing in their original setting, and the man said, "Go ahead and pick the trees you want. We'll dig them up and we'll plant them in your yard." So I carefully selected several trees and they were dug up and planted in my yard. And then I discovered to my dismay that one of the ones I had chosen was imperfect. It had been too close to an adjacent tree; and therefore when it was dug up and separated from its companion, it had a defect in its foliage. There was a hole because they had been together. That hole wasn't visible until it was separated. That distressed me greatly, chiefly because I couldn't blame anybody but myself. I had chosen the trees, and nobody else could be held responsible for it. I couldn't forgive myself for having been so stupid as to have chosen a defective tree, until the thought came to me: "What does this mean?"

And then a whole realization opened up. What it meant was that I had here a living example of the psychological consequences of living in too great a contiguity with another for too long a time. It leaves a permanent hole in the psyche to do that. This poor tree that looked fine, as long as it was right next to another tree, had this defect when it was separated from its brother or sister. When that dawned on me my feeling went out to that poor tree, that had had that traumatic experience, and I actually loved it more than the perfect ones. And the whole thing was resolved. And at the

---

[27] *Nature*, p. 3.

same time I thought I had an insight into the nature of things as the result of that experience. I think that was a "burying the loincloth" type of experience for me, analogous to that of Jeremiah. We all have experiences like that, all the time, if we can only apply the questioning attitude to them, "Now what does this mean? Why did Yahweh put me up to this?" That's my point.

There is another example of that phenomenon in chapter 16, where Yahweh says to Jeremiah:

> You must not take a wife or have son or daughter in this place. For Yahweh says this regarding the sons and daughters to be born in this place, about the mothers who give birth to them, and about the fathers who beget them in this land: They will die of deadly diseases, unlamented and unburied; they will be like dung spread on the ground; they will meet their end by sword and famine, and their corpses will be food for the birds of heaven and the beasts of earth. (16:2-4)

So the message is then that you, Jeremiah, are singled out and different. You're not going to share the general fate. You are not to participate in the biological destiny of your fellow man. You're to be spared and not participate in the general ruin.

Considering this as an archetypal image, it is a grave and ambiguous matter when we try to apply it to actual life experience. Two alternative possibilities come to my mind about it. One I think of is the case of Kierkegaard. He is thought of as the founder of modern existentialism. He was not permitted by his unconscious to marry his dearly beloved woman, Regina. It was the tragedy of his life, that although he loved her dearly and she wanted to be married, he was not permitted by his unconscious to marry. The consequence of this, in my reading of his life, is that this allowed him to fulfill his prophetic function to the modern world which I don't think would have happened if he had married, if his libido had gone in that domestic direction. So I think of Kierkegaard as a kind of modern example of Jeremiah who was not permitted to participate in the general biological destiny.

But now we also have a lot of young people in contemporary times who anticipate ecological catastrophe or something of the sort and therefore decide to have no children, decide that they're going to avoid that collective biological responsibility. I think in many cases this is a regressive evasion of responsibility that prolongs immaturity. And this would be an example of the misapplication of that particular archetypal pattern. Certainly in my experience there is nothing more effective in challenging one's own childishness than becoming a parent. If there are real children around one can't get away with being a child oneself anymore.

Another item comes from chapter 19. Yahweh says to Jeremiah:

> Go and buy an earthenware jug. Take some of the elders of the people and some priests with you. . . . You are to break this jug in front of the men who are with you, and say to them, Yahweh Sabaoth says this: I am going to break this people and this city just as one breaks a potter's pot, irreparably."
> (19:1-2, 10-11)

I think one way of reading this story is that the event came first and the explanation came after. At least that's the way it often happens psychologically. If the event came first, what would have happened would be that Jeremiah succumbed to a fit of rage in which he broke some crockery as he was raging against some elders. And then when he reflected afterward, "What does this mean?" understanding might come. That is the way it often happens to people now. It happens in reverse. You have the experience first and then you have to try to understand the meaning of being possessed by the affect. And what the statement of Yahweh conveys psychologically is that what is expressed at first as an apparently personal reaction contains a collective, archetypal content which is communicating a general meaning.

For instance, it might be that Jeremiah was initially quite chagrined at having lost his temper and behaving, apparently, irrationally—until Yahweh pointed out to him that that wasn't your rage, Jeremiah, it was mine and you were performing a function for me. As one comes to understand the affects that well up from within as having that archetypal source, it gives one a whole different attitude toward one's emotional reactions.

This particular episode with Jeremiah is somewhat reminiscent of a frustrated, neglected wife who might start throwing dishes. If that event were to be examined it might very well be discovered that the apparently personal reaction isn't personal at all. The offended goddess is throwing the dishes, you see, and it takes on a whole different import when that archetypal dimension is recognized.

However this is a kind of touchy business if archetypal energies are flowing through one. And it brings up the whole matter of the dangers of being a prophet or of the prophetic function. The specific danger is identification with the divine message and the divine affect. Another part of it is the problem that if one is expressing archetypal energies or messages, one is still a human being in a human situation and has to take the consequences of one's behavior. This often means taking the blame for being the bearer of bad news. That's a well-known phenomenon for analysts. None of us likes to be the bearer of bad tidings, because in olden times such people would sometimes get killed on the spot, because they announced the defeat of an army or something like that. And that is something analysts have to do too: they have to draw attention to the shadow; they have to be the bearer of bad news, and that has consequences.

This matter of identification comes up very explicitly in the accounts of Jeremiah. There is really quite a dialogue that takes place between Jeremiah and Yahweh. In some places it almost seems like a prototype of Job. Let me read you a little bit. This is from chapter 12; Jeremiah is talking:

> You have right on your side, Yahweh,
> when I complain about you.
> But I would like to debate a point of justice with you.
> Why is it that the wicked live so prosperously?
> Why do scoundrels enjoy peace?
> You plant them, they take root,
> and flourish, and even bear fruit.
> You are always on their lips,
> yet so far from their hearts.
> You know me, Yahweh, you see me,
> you probe my heart, it is in your hands.
> Drag them off like sheep for the slaughter-house,
> reserve them for the day of butchery. (12:1-3)

Yahweh replies to this:

> If you find it exhausting to race against men on foot,
> how will you compete against horses?
> If you are not secure in a peaceful country,
> how will you manage in the thickets along the Jordan? (12:5)

Now that's a little enigmatic. I think what Yahweh means there is that if you can't bear the aberrations of human behavior, how do you expect to deal with God? That's how I read that anyway.

But what's going on here is that Jeremiah is presuming to make Yahweh the instrument of his personal revenge—deriving from shadow projections. He's annoyed that the wicked prosper, you see. That's a shadow projection. And he wants revenge on the wicked for having a better time of it than he does, even though he's righteous. That is an example of identification with his message.

Then there's an extraordinary passage in chapter 20. Jeremiah says:

> You have seduced me, Yahweh, and I have let myself be seduced;
> you have overpowered me: you were the stronger.
> I am a daily laughing stock,
> everybody's butt,
> Each time I speak the word, I have to howl
> and proclaim: "Violence and ruin!"
> The word of Yahweh has meant for me
> insult, derision, all day long.
> I used to say, "I will not think about him,
> I will not speak in his name any more."
> Then there seemed to be a fire burning in my heart,
> imprisoned in my bones.
> The effort to restrain it wearied me,
> I could not bear it. (20:7-9)

This gives us, really, a splendid insight into the psychological experience of Jeremiah. The unconscious, or Yahweh's message manifesting itself through Jeremiah's affects, insisted on being given expression and could not be held back, because it was like a fire burning in his heart.

A small parallel that one encounters sometimes is that there will be shy, retiring people in analysis who tend not to participate very much, to take a back seat and not express themselves freely in groups. The time may come when they have strong reactions and discover that fire burning in their hearts; they want to express something and their bones are on fire very much the way Jeremiah describes it. In that situation they are analogous to Jeremiah. Their own psychological development, prompted by the Self, is requiring of them a greater degree of participation, a greater degree of expression, demanding that they accept at least a small version of the prophetic function, just as Jeremiah was obliged to do. But he had to do it on a large scale, and when it came out of him it came out of him in howls as he says here. He was probably almost psychotic during his possession by the word of Yahweh.

Prophesying and Psychosis

Indeed the whole archetype of the prophet is a common content of the psychoses. I can give you a personal example of that. This comes from a patient I saw when I was working at Rockland State Hospital many years ago, in 1954 as a matter of fact. Here is the way I described the patient upon admission.

> Twenty-four old slender blond man. He was a minister. The story was that his difficulties began about three weeks ago when he was serving as a minister for three rural churches in upstate New York. At this time he began hearing auditory hallucinations of God, telling him that he was the Messiah, the second coming of Christ. He states that he fought against this message and carried on conversations with God, insisting that this could not be. God, however, told him that at the very least he must take this information to the churches and convey it to them. And while describing this he is rather apologetic and sheepish, knowing perfectly well that this is an insane idea. However he had definite ideas of reference. For example he had attached unusual significance to a movie he saw. It was a movie involving the commander of a submarine. The patient felt that this was a symbolic picture of his life. The submarine represented the church. The sea was the sea of life. And the patient thought of himself as the commander. The message conveyed by this movie was that in the end the submarine will reach its destination and all will be well, although there will be many difficulties in the meantime. He states he considers himself a coward, believes he is too much a coward to return to his previous job and support his wife as he should. He would rather stay here with the patients than go back and face his work.

Well, he wasn't really as good as this sounds. He was delusional and assaultive, so he had to be confined on the violent ward. I made a record some days later from that ward:

> He is quite confused in thinking, still receiving messages from God that he is the second coming of Christ. Sometimes he wants to march out of the hospital and start preaching the message. The messages come from the wind and from the birds when they fly down and flutter their feathers. At the same time he feels himself to be cowardly and unable to take a stand.

That's an example of being overcome by the prophet archetype and falling into an overt psychosis. There is evidence in Jeremiah that he lived right on the brink of that kind of phenomenon. Because the archetypal image is terribly powerful. He speaks specifically, Jeremiah does, about fighting against being Yahweh's instrument. And this is very similar to the way this patient spoke against his so-called crazy idea. When the ego is weak and cannot take such a powerful archetypal dynamism symbolically, then it falls victim to its concrete manifestation. That's what happens in the case of psychosis, because one falls victim to the literal idea, and then one *is* crazy.

You see, in chapter 20 Jeremiah complains of having his relation to his fellow man destroyed because he is the bringer of bad news. He was put in the stocks for howling this bad news to his fellow Israelites. Now one reason that that sort of thing will happen is that the prophet tends to identify with Yahweh's anger. He lives it out. When that's done, he loses his relatedness to other people; he fails to take into account their reality. He fails to adapt his message, to mediate it to the psychological reality of those he is talking to. When he does that he is so grossly offensive to others that he calls down reprisals on himself. But even at the very best, even at the most careful, it can be very dangerous to be a prophet—if one tells all that one sees or intuits.

There are a couple of other images I want to mention. One is a striking description of Yahweh's reaction to Israel, in the way a husband reacts to an unfaithful wife. Yahweh is speaking through Jeremiah:

> If a man divorces his wife
> and she leaves him
> to marry someone else,
> may she still go back to him?
> Has not that piece of land
> been totally polluted?
> And you, who have prostituted yourself with so many lovers,
> you would come back to me?—it is Yahweh who speaks.
>
> Lift your eyes to the bare heights and look!
> Is there a single place where you have not offered your body?
> You waited by the roadside for your clients
> like an Arab in the desert.
> You have polluted the country
> with your prostitution and your vices:
> this is why the showers have been withheld,
> the late rains have not come.
>
> And you maintained a prostitute's bold front,
> never thinking to blush. (3:1-3)

This gives us a very interesting insight into the archetypal image behind sexual jealousy. You know that can be one of the most powerful passions known to us under certain circumstances. This particular passage would suggest that what lies behind such intense emotion is the wrath of the Self at the violation or breaking of faith in the connection between the ego and the Self. In other words, if the whole God-human connection, or ego-Self connection, is projected onto the beloved, which is what happens in some cases, then the unfaithfulness of the loved one evokes Yahweh's wrath against Israel, or the Self's wrath against the infidelity of the ego. It gives us another whole dimension of understanding that phenomenon.

One final image. In chapter 5 Yahweh says to Jeremiah:

> Rove to and fro through the streets of Jerusalem,
> look, now, and learn,
> search her squares;
> if you can find a man,
> one man who does right
> and seeks the truth,
> then I will pardon her,
> says Yahweh. (5:1)

Here we have the idea that one just person can redeem the whole city. Now if you translate that into psychological terms it raises the hypothetical idea that one really individuated person might just possibly redeem the human race. We don't know how many it would take to do that, but there is evidence that if there are enough it can happen. Anyway, I believe that kind of thinking is appropriate to us who do our daily work with single individuals in spite of the fact that the world is made up of billions. It's a kind of counterbalance to collective thinking.

4
Jeremiah, Part Two

It seems to me that Jeremiah is the most powerful figure in the Old Testament. To my mind the Book of Jeremiah is unique in the personal, psychological dimension that it reveals. The profound, agonizing conflict that Jeremiah experienced concerning his vocation, his mission and the terrible ordeal that it subjected him to, is expressed so explicitly that he really joins hands with us. He's a modern in that sense. It's a psychological account that we can understand. He had no personal life. Everything was sacrificed to his mission. It was an agony to him.

As I was thinking about it today the thought came to me: it's just conceivable that Jeremiah could have written the Book of Job. I've never heard such an idea before, it just came out of me. But it's of that same quality. And as far as I'm concerned it's possible.

Tonight we're going to review chapters 26-52. I have decided to order my remarks around three major images that come up in this portion of Jeremiah. They are: 1) the act of faith exemplified by his buying a field when Jerusalem was under siege; 2) the image of the golden cup of divine wrath; and 3) the theme of the two covenants, because a new covenant is announced—so that we have the theme of the old covenant and the new.

Purchasing a Field

The symbolic act of purchasing a field is described in chapter 32, where Jeremiah says:

> The word of Yahweh has been addressed to me as follows, "Look, Hanamel the son of your uncle Shallum will come to you and say: Buy my field at Anathoth, for you have the right of redemption to purchase it." And, as Yahweh had said, my cousin Hanamel came to me. . . . He said to me, "Buy my field at Anathoth, for you have the right of inheritance and redemption. . . ." I knew then that this was Yahweh's order. [It's as though it were a synchronistic experience.] Accordingly I bought the field . . . and paid him the price: seventeen silver shekels. I drew up the deed and sealed it, called in witnesses and weighed out the money. . . . I . . . handed over the deed of purchase to Baruch [his secretary] . . . in the presence of . . . witnesses who had signed the deed of purchase, and of all the Jews who then happened to

be in the Court of the Guard. In their presence I gave Baruch these instructions: Take these deeds, the sealed deed of purchase and its open copy, and put them in an earthenware pot, so that they may be preserved for a long time. For Yahweh Sabaoth, the God is Israel, says this, People will buy fields and vineyards in this land again. (32:6-15)

This is really quite an astonishing event when one considers the context. The city was ready to fall under siege, and yet this act of faith in its restitution was lived out.

What it amounts to, if we just take the image in its literal aspect, is that God orders Jeremiah to invest in the earth. I would understand that as a command for *coagulatio*—to invest one's libido in a piece of concrete earth. In other words, to demonstrate faith in the material, ego existence, not to withdraw into the spirit but to commit one's energy to this doomed world of the besieged Jerusalem. One reason this parabolic action attracts my interest is that it brings up the whole archetypal theme of trust in God, faith in the ultimate meaning of existence. It refers to a demonstrated loyalty to life that prevents one from defecting to the renegade attitude of nihilism.

This theme comes up in many passages in the Old Testament. I have gleaned just a few examples to give you the flavor of the sentiment that's expressed:

> Though he slay me, yet will I trust in him. (Job 13:15, AV)

> Offer the sacrifices of righteousness, And put your trust in the Lord. (Ps. 4:5, NKJV)

> O my God, I trust in thee: let me not be ashamed, let not mine enemies triumph over me. (Ps. 25:2, AV)

> Many sorrows shall be to the wicked: but he that trusteth in the Lord, mercy shall compass him about. (Ps. 32:10, AV)

> For our heart shall rejoice in him, because we have trusted in his holy name. (Ps. 33:21, AV)

> Trust in the Lord with all thine heart; and lean not unto thine own understanding. In all thy ways acknowledge him, and he shall direct thy paths. (Prov. 3:5-6, AV)

And then finally,

> Whoso trusteth in the Lord, happy is he. (Prov. 16:20, AV)

Later on, the Apostle Paul picked up this theme of faith in a major way. He developed the whole notion that was then further elaborated in Protestantism, namely justification by faith. The most important text on this is found in his Letter to the Romans. Let me read you a little portion:

> We know that everything the law says is addressed to those who are under its authority. This means that every mouth is silenced and the whole world stands convicted before God, since no one will be justified in God's sight through observance of the law; the law does nothing but point out what is sinful.
>
> But now the justice of God has been manifested apart from the law, even though both law and prophets bear witness to it—that justice of God which works though faith in Jesus Christ for all who believe. All men of sin that are deprived of the glory of God. All men are now undeservedly justified by the gift of God through the redemption wrought in Christ Jesus. Through his blood God made him the means of expiation for all who believe [the literal translation would read "through faith in his blood"] so that he might be just and might justify those who believe in Jesus. (3:19-26, NAB)

The emphasis here, you see, the requirement, is what's translated as belief, but it's the word *pistis,* or a variant of that stem, which means faith.

This whole archetypal idea of faith has been so distorted and so misused that I see it as a great archetypal image that has been damaged almost beyond repair for the modern mind. It has come to mean blind, unreflecting belief that represses its opposite, namely doubt, and thus generates fanatics who project their doubt onto others and then attack them for that projection. During the inquisition when a heretic was burned at the stake, that was called an act of faith, so you can see the whole matter of faith has become highly problematic. That is quite a damaged archetypal image. I believe it needs to be rescued from its primitive literalism and unconscious misuse, by trying to understand it psychologically.

Following up this matter I looked into how the Catholic Church defines faith. I found this:

> We have accompanied the believer in his progress toward an act of faith until the stage at which having acquired a firm conviction concerning the preambles of faith, he forms an evident judgment of credibility. This truth which I am convinced has been revealed by God is to be believed on God's authority. Passing to a judgment of the practical order he says, "I must believe it." Then and not until then he proceeds to give his assent to the revealed truth: I believe this truth because God has revealed it. This subject is

of such vital importance that our definition of the act of faith must be taken from the infallible pronouncement of the Vatican Council. The Council directly defines the virtue of faith. But in doing so it necessarily defines the act: "Faith is a supernatural virtue whereby inspired and assisted by the grace of God we believe that the things which he has revealed are true. Not because the intrinsic truth of the thing is plainly perceived by the natural light of reason, but because of the authority of God himself who reveals them and who can who neither be deceived nor deceive."[28]

Now that's not too hard to translate psychologically. The issue of faith is based on the revelation of what God has revealed. The only question is where one finds one's revelation. Is it found in the orthodox prescribed text or in one's own experience? Psychologically we can understand this to mean that faith is loyalty to the transpersonal reality as revealed by the unconscious, by one's own experience of the depths. So it is fidelity to one's own revelation. It certainly is true that experiences of the Self bring with them a sense of conviction, therefore of faith, that what one is experiencing exists. You don't have to make an effort to believe it, because the experience itself conveys that conviction.

But we still have to account, I think, for the fact that faith is such a demanding imperative. I think what is indicated by that fact is that experiences of the Self do need continual reinforcement and remembrance—or faith of the ego—in order not to sink away again. The Self needs the faith of the ego to bear witness to its reality.

In this psychological sense one can say that one is indeed justified by faith. Because the extent to which one is loyal or faithful to the experiences of the Self one has had determines the strength of the ego's connection with the Self—which is the psychological equivalent of justification.

These are some of the implications, I think, in the symbolic action of Jeremiah buying a plot of ground even though Jerusalem was in the desperate state of being under siege. He was bearing witness not only to the existence of Yahweh but also to the ultimately meaningful and redemptive aspects of Yahweh's existence; in other words, that in the end life would prevail, in spite of the darkness of the moment. The essence of it, in the passage quoted, is the "infallible pronouncement" of the Vatican Council:

Faith is a supernatural virtue whereby inspired and assisted by the grace of God we believe that the things which he has revealed are true. Not because

---

[28] [Source unknown.—Ed.]

the intrinsic truth of the thing is plainly perceived by the natural light of reason, but because of the authority of God Himself who reveals them and who can neither be deceived nor deceive.

When things are presented in such an essentially theological way, it is very easy to make the translation to the psychological equivalent. It becomes a symbolic statement, you see.

The Vessel of Divine Wrath

I want to turn to the image of the vessel containing the divine wrath—a cup of abominations. It is a kind of negative Holy Grail. I think there are some quite important insights imbedded in this imagery which I hope to be able to extract. It shows up in Jeremiah in chapter 25, where we read:

> Yahweh the God of Israel said this to me, "Take this cup of wine from my hand and make all the nations to whom I send you drink it, let them drink and reel and lose their wits at the sword I am sending among them." I took the cup from the hand of Yahweh and made all the nations to whom Yahweh sent me drink it. [And then he describes all the places he goes.] . . .
>
> "You are to say to them, 'Yahweh Sabaoth, the God of Israel, says this: Drink! Get drunk! Vomit! Fall, never to rise, at the sword that I am sending among you! . . . You must drink! Since I am now making a beginning of disaster. . . .'
>
> "Let your prophecy to them contain all these words . . . .
>
> "Yahweh roars from on high,
>
> . . . .
>
> he roars loud against his sheepfold,
> he shouts aloud like those who tread the grape.
>
> . . . .
>
> For Yahweh is indicting the nations,
> arraigning all flesh for judgement;
> the wicked he abandons to the sword
>
> . . . .
>
> Howl, shepherds, shriek,
> roll on the ground, you lords of the flock,
> for the days have arrived for your slaughter,
> like the finest rams you will fall. . . ." (25:15-34)

—and so on, just horrible outpourings. What this passage indicates is that Jeremiah is being used by Yahweh as a cup to hold and pour out Yahweh's wrath on the nations. So Jeremiah himself becomes quite literally the vessel of divine wrath, because he is the one who is pouring out all these dire passages which quite understandably enrage people. A number of times he was almost killed by the mob.

This was the first occasion for the use of this image of the cup. But then in chapter 51 it comes up again, used in reference to Babylon:

> Yahweh says this:
> Against the citizens of Leb-kamai [that's Babylon] I will rouse
> a destroying spirit;
> I will send winnowers to Babylon to winnow her and leave her bare:
> for they will beleaguer her from every side
> in the day of disaster.
> . . . .
> —No quarter for her young warriors!
> Vow her whole army to the ban!
> In the country of the Chaldaeans the slaughtered will fall,
> in the streets of Babylon, those whom the sword runs through.
> This is because their country was full of sin
> against the Holy One of Israel.
> . . . .
> Escape out of Babylon
> (save your lives, each one of you);
> . . . .
> for this is the time of Yahweh's vengeance:
> he is paying her her reward!
> Babylon was a golden cup in Yahweh's hand,
> she made the whole world drunk,
> the nations drank her wine
> and then went mad.
> [In other words Babylon is here seen as an agent of Yahweh's wrath just as
> Jeremiah was.]
> Babylon has suddenly fallen, is broken:
> lament for her!
> Go and fetch balm for her wounds,
> perhaps she can be cured!
> —"We tried to cure Babylon; she has got no better.
> Leave her alone and let us each go to his own country."
> Yes, her sentence reaches to the sky,
> rises to the very clouds.
> Yahweh has vindicated our integrity.
> Come, let us tell in Zion
> what Yahweh our God has done.
> Sharpen the arrows,
> fill the quivers!

Yahweh has roused the spirit of the king of the Medes, because he has a plan against Babylon to destroy it; this is the vengeance of Yahweh, the revenge for his Temple. (51:1-11)

This passage reveals a terrible fact about Yahweh. Let me show you how. Other passages have made clear that Yahweh was using Babylon as his agent to punish Israel. In chapter 51 Yahweh says to Babylon:

> You were my mace [sometimes translated as hammer],
> a weapon of war.
> With you I crushed the nations,
> struck kingdoms down,
> with you crushed horse and rider,
> chariot and charioteer,
> with you crushed man and woman,
> old man and young,
> youth and maid,
> with you crushed shepherd and flock,
> plowman and team,
> governors and nobles,

but I will let you see how I make Babylon and the inhabitants of Chaldaea pay for the all the wrongs they have done to Zion. It is Yahweh who speaks. (51:20-24)

The terrible fact about Yahweh is that he uses a nation or an individual as an agent of his divine wrath, a vessel to pour out his punishing wrath on someone else, and then he holds that agent personally responsible for the actions that he, Yahweh, had made him do! That is explicit here, absolutely explicit. And it is psychologically true too.

It is a striking feature of this text that Babylon was called a golden cup in Yahweh's hand. Gold, you know, signifies supreme value. And thus this golden cup of Babylon is identified as the Self. We also encounter this image of a golden cup in Revelation:

"Come here and I will show you the punishment given to the famous prostitute who rules enthroned beside abundant waters, the one with whom all the kings of the earth have committed fornication, and who has made all the population of the world drunk with the wine of her adultery." . . . I saw a woman riding a scarlet beast which had seven heads and ten horns and had blasphemous titles written all over it. The woman was dressed in purple and scarlet, and glittered with gold and jewels and pearls, and she was holding a gold wine cup filled with the disgusting filth of her fornication; on her forehead was written a name, a cryptic name: "Babylon the Great, the mother of all the prostitutes and all the filthy practices on the earth." I saw that she was drunk, drunk with the blood of the saints, and the blood of the martyrs of Jesus. (17:1-6)

And it becomes clear as the passage goes on that this refers to Rome— at least that's the most immediate reference, there are other eschatological references too—but in so far as it refers to Rome, Rome is being equated with Babylon. And again we have a golden cup. And even though its contents are despicable, nonetheless the cup is of gold. So again we must see this as a symbol of the Self, a negative manifestation of the Self.

I think one more cup reference is relevant. In the Garden of Gethsemane, when Christ is struggling to accept his destiny of crucifixion. He says, "My father if it is possible, let this cup pass me by. Nevertheless let it be as you, not I, would have it." (Matt. 26:39) This is the same cup. It is the cup of divine wrath that Jeremiah made the nations drink by his prophesying. And it is the same cup that Babylon became. Only in this case, Christ is assimilating it rather than pouring it out.

Jung has an important remark concerning this image in *Mysterium Coniunctionis,* where he says:

> If the projected conflict is to be healed, it must return into the psyche of the individual, where it had its unconscious beginnings. He must celebrate a Last Supper with himself, and eat and drink his own flesh and drink his own blood; which means that he must recognize and accept the other in himself. . . . Is this perhaps the meaning of Christ's teaching, that each must bear his own cross? For if you have to endure yourself, how will you be able to rend others also?[29]

In a footnote to that paragraph, Jung says that the image of the drinking of the blood of the lion—this is all in an extended commentary on the image in an alchemical text of drinking lion's blood—refers to the assimilating of affects and the subjugation of concupiscence.

If we apply those remarks to our text of Jeremiah we must realize that affects and concupiscence derive from Yahweh, because it's the affect of his divine wrath that is being poured out; affects and concupiscence are the manifestations of the primitive, unregenerate Self. So that to assimilate those affects and to subjugate that concupiscence means, in essence, to

---

[29] CW 14, par. 512.

drink the contents of the cup of divine wrath rather than pour it out. And to do that brings about a transformation or humanizing of the Self.

The fact is, Yahweh needs man to take responsibility for his, Yahweh's, fiery wrath and passion, in order for him, Yahweh, to undergo transformation. I think that's all to be read quite clearly in these images.[30]

The Two Covenants

The third major image I want to talk about is that of the two covenants and Jeremiah's announcement of the new covenant. This occurs in the great thirty-first chapter of Jeremiah which begins by describing a reconciliation between Israel and Yahweh. It starts out this way:

> Yahweh says this:
> They have found pardon in the wilderness,
> those who have survived the sword.
> Israel is marching to his rest.
> Yahweh has appeared to him from afar:
> I have loved you with an everlasting love,
> so I am constant in my affection for you.
> I build you once more; you shall be rebuilt,
> virgin of Israel.
> Adorned once more, and with your tambourines,
> you will go out dancing gaily.
> You will plant vineyards once more
> on the mountains of Samaria
> (the planters have done their planting: they will gather the fruit).
> Yes, a day will come when the watchmen shout
> on the mountains of Ephraim,
> "Up! Let us go up to Zion,
> to Yahweh our God!"
>
> For Yahweh says this:
> Shout with joy for Jacob!
> Hail the chief of nations!
> Proclaim! Praise! Shout:
> "Yahweh has saved his people,
> the remnant of Israel!"
> See, I will bring them back
> from the land of the North
> and gather them from the far ends of the earth;

---

[30] [This theme is the subject of Jung's "Answer to Job," *Psychology and Religion, CW* 12; see also Edinger, *Transformation of the God-Image.*—Ed.]

all of them: the blind and the lame,
women with child,, women in labor:
a great company returning here.
They had left in tears,
I will comfort them as I lead them back;
I will guide them to streams of water,
by a smooth path where they will not stumble.
For I am a father to Israel,
and Ephraim is my first-born son. (31:2-9)

Then Ephraim, which is a synonym for Israel, in turn replies:

You have disciplined me, I accepted the discipline
like a young bull untamed.
Bring me back, let me come back,
for you are Yahweh my God!
Yes, I turned away, but have since repented. (31:18-19)

The reference to the disciplining of a young bull reminds us of the symbolic story of the yoke that was presented in chapter 27. We were told there that Yahweh required Jeremiah to wear a yoke around his neck, to go about in that condition, in order to symbolize the fact that the nations must submit to the yoke of Nebuchadnezzar whom Yahweh here speaks of as "my servant." But because Israel would not submit willingly to the yoke of Babylon, it was subjected to the harsher yoke of the exile.

The image of yoking or disciplining a young bull is an image of taming. There is another example of this archetypal image in hexagram 26 of the *I Ching*. The title of it is "The Taming Power of the Great." The commentaries on the lines of that hexagram speak of such things as the gelding of a boar or the fastening of a headboard against a young bull's horns to prevent them from growing out. The image of this hexagram also speaks of the strengthening of character, in these words:

The superior man acquaints himself with many sayings of antiquity and many deeds of the past in order to strengthen his character thereby. . . . In the words and deeds of the past there lies hidden a treasure that men may use to strengthen and elevate their own characters. The way to study the past is not to confine oneself to mere knowledge of history but, through application of this knowledge, to give actuality to the past.[31]

I think, in a very interesting way, a very quiet way, that the *I Ching*

---

[31] Richard Wilhelm, trans., *The I Ching or Book of Changes,* p. 105.

here links the taming of wild animals with the process of human culture—which is a civilizing, domesticating process that tames raw human energies by pitting them against historical and cultural facts. This has the effect of reminding the individual that he or she is not the first and only person to come into existence. And the net result of the acculturating process is a taming of the instincts.

But now that Israel has accepted the discipline of the exile, now that she has accepted the yoke of Yahweh, she has found pardon in the wilderness. Yahweh says in the thirtieth chapter:

> On that day . . . I will break the yoke on their necks, and snap their chains. They will be no longer the servants of aliens, but will serve Yahweh their God. (30:8)

In other words, servitude to man will be replaced by servitude to God.

Psychologically, this would mean that the ego has reached the realization that all constriction and limitation is from the Self. The yoke of necessity is actually the yoke of Yahweh. Acquiring such a religious attitude releases the ego from kicking against the goad, and, like the Israelites in exile, it can find pardon in the wilderness.

Every source of anxiety and frustration in one's personal life, if it's traced back far enough, will be found to derive from the Self. If one is beset with various fears—crime in the streets, or theft, or the tax authorities, any of a number of things—if you trace that fear back behind its immediate, apparent reference, you will see that it comes from the Self. When that can be so realized, it turns into the fear of God, which is the beginning of wisdom. Then you can be thankful for having it, you see, rather than feeling it as a plague.

That's the way you find pardon in the wilderness: when you find a religious attitude toward your symptom.

There is a beautiful expression of this religious attitude of acceptance in Emerson's essay entitled "Experience." He says this:

> We should not postpone and refer and wish, but do broad justice where we are, by whomsoever we deal with, accepting our actual companions and circumstances, however humble or odious, as the mystic officials to whom the universe has delegated its whole pleasure for us.[32]

It's the same idea.

---

[32] *Essays,* p. 304.

So with Israel's new attitude, she is restored to Yahweh's good graces. And Yahweh, in turn, makes a magnificent promise:

See, the days are coming—it is Yahweh who speaks—when I am going to sow the seed of men and cattle on the House of Israel and on the House of Judah. And as I once watched them to tear up, to knock down, to overthrow, destroy and bring disaster, so now I shall watch over them to build and to plant. It is Yahweh who speaks.

In those days people will no longer say:

"The fathers have eaten unripe grapes;
the children's teeth are set on edge."

But each is to die for his own sin. Every man who eats unripe grapes is to have his own teeth set on edge.

See, the days are coming—it is Yahweh who speaks—when I will make a new covenant with the house of Israel (and the house of Judah), but not a covenant like the one I made with their ancestors on the day I took them by the hand to bring them out of the land of Egypt. They broke that covenant of mine, so I had to show them who was master. It is Yahweh who speaks. No, this is the covenant I will make with the house of Israel when those days arrive—it is Yahweh who speaks. Deep within then I will plant my Law, writing it on their hearts. Then I will be their God and they shall be my people. There will be no further need for neighbor to try to teach neighbor, or brother to say to brother, "Learn to know Yahweh!" No, they will all know me, the least no less than the greatest—it is Yahweh who speaks—since I will forgive their iniquity and never call their sin to mind. (31:27-34)

To put this statement in context I would just like to recall the sequence of events that this is the last of. It all started with the Jews in bondage in Egypt. They were rescued by Yahweh through Moses, given the Law on Mount Sinai and had the first or old covenant established between Yahweh and Israel. They arrived in the promised land and their nation grew and prospered. And the old covenant was more and more disregarded and eventually this led to the punishment, exile in the wilderness. But then through that experience of utter and total defeat a change of mind, a *metanoia*, took place—a reconciliation. And the fruit or consequence of that reconciliation was the announcement of this new covenant which speaks of an inner Law, an inner knowledge of Yahweh, a totally different kind of experience than the first covenant.

This theme of two covenants, the old and the new, has undergone a lot of development. It's been picked up in various places, and the collective psyche has enlarged it and unfolded it in various ways. One example: In the first century before Christ a community of Essenes, the Qumran community, the ones the Dead Sea Scrolls belonged to, attributed great importance to the theme of the two covenants. They considered that the promise of the new covenant in the thirty-first chapter of Jeremiah had been fulfilled in their midst. And they called themselves the new covenant in the land of Damascus. So while the Sinai covenant was for the whole people, the Qumran covenanters considered themselves to be its holy remnant, the pure eschatological community of the age of salvation. This explains their strict rules for receiving new members and certain other facts, such as their sex thinking on the covenant, which distinguished them especially from the Rabbis, who equated the covenant with circumcision and saw its preservation guaranteed by a rigorous keeping of the Mosaic Law. So that's one place where the new covenant blossomed as a collective psychic reality.

Of course the place where it received its greatest development was in Christianity. The whole New Testament that has been tacked on to the Old Testament is the new covenant. That might be a more accurate term for it. Testament and covenant are synonymous. So it is books of the new covenant that have been tacked onto the books of the old covenant. This is expressed perhaps most clearly in the Letter to the Hebrews, which was once thought to have been written by Paul, though that is very unlikely. Anyway, in the eighth and ninth chapters of Hebrews this passage of Jeremiah concerning the new covenant is quoted in full and then applied to Christ. I'll read a bit of it to give you the feel of it:

> The blood of goats and bulls and the ashes of a heifer are sprinkled on those who have incurred defilement and they restore the holiness of their outward lives; how much more effectively the blood of Christ, who offered himself as the perfect sacrifice to God . . . can purify our inner self from dead actions so that we do our service to the living God.
>
> He brings a new covenant, as the mediator, only so that the people who were called to an eternal inheritance may actually receive what was promised: his death took place to cancel the sins that infringed the earlier covenant. (9:13-15)

And then it goes on to speak of the blood of the old covenant, the blood of animals which sealed the old covenant, and refers to the blood of Christ being shed as the blood of the new covenant. So this archetypal image has undergone a major development in Christian symbolism.

Then nothing much came of it for many centuries. The Church Fathers didn't do very much more with it beyond what Paul said, but with the onset of Protestantism it's as though it received another lease on life. The theological fantasies of Calvinism and Puritanism picked it up and there developed what was called a covenant theology. According to this scheme, God at the creation entered into an agreement with Adam as the federal head of the race, promising to him and his descendants eternal life, on condition of his obedience to the divine command that he should not eat of the fruit of the Tree of Knowledge of Good and Evil, threatening him with eternal death for himself and his descendants if he disobeyed.

But Adam failed to stand the test. So God entered into a second agreement with Christ as the second Adam, on behalf of the elect, promising them forgiveness and eternal life in consideration of Christ's perfect obedience and satisfaction imputed to them by faith, as well as all the gifts and graces which are necessary to the realization of this supreme blessing in experience. So this covenant theology in its developed form is a doctrine in which the entire system of divinity is expressed in terms of these two covenants. Our assurance of salvation is based upon the fact that we are included within that latter covenant.

This is enough, I think, to demonstrate that this is an archetypal image that can manifest itself in various ways with considerable power. And so we must ask ourselves what this archetypal image of the two covenants means psychologically.

I think the first covenant would refer to the experience of the first half of life in which the Self is encountered chiefly in projection onto parents and society and the outer authority or literal creedal religion. Or to the introjects of those externalizations, what is called the superego. Those make up the first covenant, namely the original sense of connection between the ego and the Self—which is not an immediate inner one, but is mediated by external factors and based on projections and concrete externalizations.

But sooner or later, if the developmental process is to proceed the full way, that first covenant breaks down. There is a transition period where there's a breakdown of the projections of the Self which had kept the ego intact before: the loss of religious belief, or loss of trust in the external carriers of the authority projections, leading to a sense of despair and alienation, opening the ego to an onslaught from the unconscious. And if that transition period is survived, it can lead over to the second half of life, into what is symbolized by the new, second covenant, where a recovery of connection with the Self takes place on a different level. The Self is now experienced as an inner individual reality through one's direct living experience. And then the words of Jeremiah will be quite strictly and literally applicable, namely:

> There will be no further need for neighbor to try to teach neighbor, or brother to say to brother, "Learn to know Yahweh!" No, they will all know me. (31:34)

5
Lamentations; Ezekiel, Part One

Lamentations

As is indicated in only a few Biblical translations, one of which is the Jerusalem Bible, the Book of Lamentations is actually comprised of five acrostic poems, each one made up of twenty-two verses to include the whole Hebrew alphabet in sequence; so the first verse starts with *aleph,* the second with *bet,* the third with *gimel* and so on. We find the same phenomenon in Psalm 119. This brings up the whole question of what we might understand the meaning of an acrostic to be.

A simple example of an acrostic is a word square, where the words read the same vertically and horizontally:

C R A B
R A R E
A R T S
B E S T

It tickles the child in one to discover another dimension of meaning or communication beyond the immediately evident one. On a deeper level, I think what it symbolizes is the revelation of another dimension of existence that shows through or can be perceived beyond the everyday, apparent level of existence. On the surface of it, we have a series of laments for the defeat of Jerusalem. But shining through them is the sequence of the Hebrew alphabet, which carries a certain mysterious significance when it manifests on another level.

Now the Hebrew alphabet has been the subject of all sorts of what I would call cosmogonic fantasies. According to the Cabbala the twenty-two letters of the Hebrew alphabet, together with the first ten numbers, were used to create the world. To get some feel for this mystical aspect of the Hebrew alphabet I want to draw your attention to a delightful little book by Lawrence Kushner concerning the Hebrew letters. I shall read you a few lines because he is rather remarkable in that he conveys, even though he is contemporary, something of the mystical feeling that actually belongs to the Cabbalists. He says:

There are a few things about the letters of the Hebrew alphabet or the Sefer OTiYOT it will help you to know.

The Sefer OTiYOT exist independently of ink and paper or even words. We learn that when Moses shattered the first set of tablets, the letters ascended to the One who gave them. And in another place, the story is told of Rabbi Hananya ben Teradyon that he was wrapped in a scroll of the Tora and burned at the stake. Moments before his death, his students cried out, "Master! What do you see?" He answered, "The parchment is burning but the letters are flying toward the heavens!"

The Sefer OTiYOT have been around since before the creation of the world and are mysteriously linked with the creative process itself. It is told of the master builder of the wilderness tabernacle . . . that he knew how to combine the letters by which the heavens and earth were made. And elsewhere we read that one of the last things God did before He rested on the seventh day . . . was to determine the precise shape of the letters.

. . . They are themselves holy. They are vessels carrying within the light of the Boundless One. [That's straight out of the Cabbala.][33]

When we think of the symbolic, mystical implications of the letters of the Hebrew alphabet, then the fact that the Lamentations are an acrostic of the alphabet takes on added significance. Since each of the five Lamentations covers the entire alphabet, each poem becomes an expression of the totality of the creative units of the world. Thus the poem itself becomes a vessel that can hold the grief being expressed, so to speak. It becomes an archetypal vessel, pointing to a larger significance than the personal defeat the inhabitants of Jerusalem were experiencing at that time.

Another thing I'd like to mention is the whole significance of the process of lamenting, especially as a ritual or structured phenomenon. There's good evidence to indicate that tragedy, what began as Greek tragedy, originated with a four-stage ritual drama concerning the life and death of the year spirit. The first stage was an *agone* or contest between the protagonist and the powers of evil, the darkness. There was then a *pathos* or defeat of the protagonist, because he succumbed to the powers of evil. The third phase was called a *threnos,* or lamentation, in which grief over the defeat of the hero was given dramatic and ritualized expression. The fourth and final phase of the dramatic sequence was a *theophany* in which some manifestation of the divine appeared and resolved the state of de-

---

[33] *Sefer OTiYOT (The Book of Letters): A Mystical Alef-bait,* pp. 4f.

spair caused by the defeat of the hero. The whole sequence shifted to another level and spiritual triumph took the place of concrete defeat.

This archetypal pattern has many examples. It was this sequence that was annually enacted in the weeping each spring for the young god Tammuz. The whole sequence of the Christian Easter cycle derives in part from that earlier death and lamentation of the son-lover of the Great Mother who then, through a divine manifestation, resurrects.

It is quite understandable psychologically, then, that the Book of Lamentations, which was originally written to express the grief of the defeat of Jerusalem, is used by the Catholic Church in the liturgy of Easter week. Because it's archetypally suitable.

I think it's also a reminder of the psychological fact that the full expression of grief is an absolutely vital part of the process of assimilating the experience of a defeat or a loss of any kind. Certainly the analyst is quite familiar with the fact that in so many cases there have been early traumatic experiences, really vital losses, that are never fully assimilated because the mourning process was arrested. The experience remains as a kind of festering complex until it can be contacted again. Then we have the remarkable phenomenon of again and again experiencing the patient's living grief over something that may have happened twenty or thirty years ago, but never went through the full process of lamentation.

Ezekiel

I want to spend most of my time tonight talking about the major vision in the first chapter of Ezekiel. But before I turn to that I want to draw your attention to several other matters that seem to warrant at least brief psychological notes. In the second chapter Yahweh says to Ezekiel:

> "Open your mouth and eat what I am about to give you." . . . He unrolled it in front of me, it was written on back and front; on it was written "lamentations, wailings, moanings." He said, "Son of man, eat what is given to you; eat this scroll, then go and speak to the House of Israel." I opened my mouth; he gave me the scroll to eat and said, "Son of man, feed and be satisfied by the scroll I am giving you." I ate it, and it tasted sweet as honey. (2:8-3:3)

This passage reminds me of the fairly common dream image of being given something to eat. A dream of that sort indicates that something is ready to be assimilated and, in almost all cases, one should accept it and eat it—even though often it doesn't look very tasty. Certainly that's the case here, because what Ezekiel is being asked to eat is grief and lamentation. The remarkable thing is that as soon as he accepts it, takes it in, it tastes sweet.

That's an indication of the fact that when one accepts something that is painful and difficult and with the attitude that one is going to assimilate it, it usually then does change its taste. From being something very bitter and painful, as it's assimilated it becomes a source of a certain satisfaction. I think it is safe to say that just about every experience that brings great pain and mourning is, when assimilated, something one would not willingly part with because it brings a sense of depth, of substance, a sense of meaning and worth. It turns out to be a precious experience. The very experiences that are most painful are those that are sweetest when assimilated. I think that's what's alluded to in this passage.

In chapter three, Yahweh says to Ezekiel:

> If I say to a wicked man: You are to die, and you do not warn him; if you do not speak and warn him to renounce his evil ways and so live, then he shall die for his sin, but I will hold you responsible for his death. (3:18)

That's a hard statement. I think it refers to the psychological fact that consciousness brings responsibility. A moral responsibility really does come with awareness. I think that's why consciousness is not very popular. If there is something dubious going on, you know, we'd rather not know about it, because then we can't be witnesses and can't be held accountable. But once we do see something and are aware of it, then we are responsible for acting on what we are aware of. If we fail to do that, then the unconscious turns negative, so to speak. In other words, Yahweh holds one responsible for what one sees and knows.

There is another image I draw to your attention because it comes up in dreams occasionally. In chapter 9 a man in white with the ink horn of a scribe is directed to go through the city making a cross on the forehead of those to be saved. And then swordsmen follow him and execute all those who do not have the mark on their forehead. What one immediately thinks of here is the mark of Cain that we read about in the fourth chapter of Genesis. Yahweh put a mark on Cain's forehead to warn those who might kill him. So the mark was meant to indicate that he was to be spared. In dreams, the image of being marked almost always indicates that the dreamer has reached a certain stage of the individuation process where an

election or a being set apart has definitively taken place, though it is ambiguous in its nature. It's not all good. It also has a dark aspect, and that's
indicated by the amplification of the mark of Cain.

Another significant image is in chapter 12. Here Yahweh orders
Ezekiel to pack an exile's bundle and to emigrate from where he is to
someplace else while his neighbors are watching. And Yahweh says,

> As they watch, you will shoulder your pack and go out into the dark; you
> will cover your face so that you cannot see the country, since I have made
> you a symbol for the House of Israel. (12:6)

So here Ezekiel the prophet is ordered to function as a symbol for the collective. In his own personal, individual life he must live out the *Zeitgeist,*
the collective experience, that is in store for the group as a whole.

I think we can apply this phenomenon to prophets in all ages. I think a
good example of that would be Nietzsche. He discovered the death of God
and fell into an inflation from it and I think his whole life, really, is a kind
of symbol for the house of Western civilization, just as Ezekiel's actions
were a symbol for the house of Israel. And, to a lesser extent, whenever an
individual has an encounter with the collective unconscious, he begins to
perceive that his personal experience corresponds to and is symbolic of the
society as a whole. He then can perceive his own life and his own experience as symbols for the house of the Western psyche, so to speak.

The same interpretation, I think, can be applied to another passage
where Yahweh says to Ezekiel, "Son of man, you are to tremble as you eat
your bread and to behave restlessly and anxiously as you drink your water" (12:18)—once again to symbolize the fact that Israel as a whole was
about to endure mass anxiety. I think a great deal of modern neurosis and
modern anxiety belongs to just that same nature: it is a phenomenon of the
collective condition, of being without a containing myth, and therefore of
being in a state of anxious exile.

The Throne-Chariot Vision

Now I want to turn to the major vision of Ezekiel found in chapter 1. If
we think of the Old Testament as a grand record of a collective, historical
individuation process, then this great mandala vision of Ezekiel's would
be the culmination of that process. If we try to draw a parallel between the
Old Testament record and the psychological process of an individual, this
vision is the culminating point where the most complex and deepest mani-

festation of the *numinosum* appears, and it is in the form that Jung has taught us to expect, namely the mandala.

Here is Ezekiel's vision:

> There the hand of Yahweh came on me. I looked; a stormy wind blew from the north, a great cloud with light around it, a fire from which flashes of lightning darted, and in the center a sheen like bronze at the heart of the fire. In the center I saw what seemed four animals. . . . They were of human form. Each had four faces, each had four wings. Their legs were straight; they had hoofs like oxen, glittering like polished brass. Human hands showed under their wings; the faces . . . were turned to the four quarters. . . . As to what they looked like, they had human faces, and all four had a lion's face to the right, . . . a bull's face to the left, and . . . an eagle's face. . . . [And there were wings], two wings that covered [the] body; and . . . they did not turn as they moved.
>
> [There were] flaming brands or torches, darting between the animals; the fire flashed . . . and lightning streaked. . . . And the creatures ran to and fro like thunderbolts.
>
> [And there was a wheel on the ground by each of the animals.] The wheels glittered as if made of chrysolite. . . . They went forward four ways and kept their course unswervingly. Their rims seemed enormous . . . and all four rims had eyes all the way around. [The wheels went with the animals when they moved as the spirit urged them] since the spirit of the animals was in the wheels. . . . Over the heads of the animals a sort of vault, gleaming like crystal, arched above their heads . . . I heard the noise of their wings as they moved; it sounded like rushing water . . . noise like a storm, like the noise of a camp. . . .
>
> Above the vault over their heads was something that looked like a sapphire; it was shaped like a throne and high up on this throne was a being that looked like a man. I saw him shine like bronze, and close to and all around him from what seemed his loins upward was what looked like fire, and from . . . his loins downward I saw what looked like fire . . . like a bow in the clouds on rainy days. . . . I looked, and prostrated myself, and I heard a voice speaking. It said, "Son of man, stand up." (1:4-2:1)

And then there were further instructions.

That's the vision. What makes it so important, when one traces out its consequences, is how basic it is to the Western psyche. The four animals derive, at least in part, from the so-called four sons of Horus (opposite). The imagery of this vision was taken over into Christian symbolism in the four animals, and the four aspects became the four evangelists who

Osiris, with the four sons of Horus on the lotus (left).
(Papyrus of Hunefer, from E.A.W. Budge, *The Book of the Dead,* 1899;
in CW 12, fig. 102.)

represented the four Gospels that were pillars of the throne of Christ.

In Jewish mysticism the throne-chariot of Ezekiel's vision became one of the central initial images, and I'm going to read a little something about that shortly. In our own day Jung has used this vision as a kind of ground plan for his most comprehensive description of the phenomenology of the Self,[34] which I will also talk about later. All this goes to show that Ezekiel's vision is really quite central to the Western psyche.

The wind and cloud announcing the vision come from the north. That's a reference to the symbolism of the north pole which was thought of as the abode of the highest Gods, because everything circled around the north pole. So it was the center. Clouds typically symbolize the manifestation of deity. I draw your attention, so far as that symbolism is concerned, to James Kirsch's book, *The Reluctant Prophet,* chapter 13, which is devoted to the symbolism of the cloud as a manifestation of the *numinosum.*

Another part of Ezekiel's vision is the fire symbolism, reflecting its intense energy. It's another aspect of divinity. That is how Yahweh manifested in the burning bush, for instance.

Then we have the phenomenon of the four animals, each with four faces. So we have four quaternities within a greater quaternity. But this imagery of the four faces, one human and three animal (lion, bull and eagle), as I said, harkens back to the four sons of Horus, one of whom had a human head while the other three were animal headed. What it indicates is that the Self, as experienced by Ezekiel, was three-quarters theriomorphic. In other words only one-fourth was humanized at that time. And that same phenomenon continued right into medieval Christianity where the symbols of the four evangelists surrounding Christ have that same proportion: three-fourths of them are animal and only one-fourth is human (opposite).

The wheels of course are explicit mandala images and the eyes on the wheels allude to the symbolism of multiple luminosities in the unconscious, in other words the existence of consciousness, perceiving consciousness, in the unconscious. So they are multiple examples of the eye of God. I imagine it would be rather disquieting to have all those eyes looking at one. Especially if one were about the size of an ant in comparison with those great images.

---

[34] [Jung: "The model of the self in *Aion* is based on the Ezekiel vision!" *Letters,* vol. 2, p. 118.—Ed.]

The four evangelists with their symbols.
(Miniature in an Evangeliary, Aschaffenburg, 13th century;
in CW 12, fig. 109.)

Then we're told that there's a great vault or dome, above which sits a throned man-like figure. I want to read to you what Jung says about that feature of Ezekiel's vision. This is from "Answer to Job." Jung had previously said that Job probably hadn't quite realized the full implications of his encounter with the Deity—that he had more consciousness than Yahweh had. The consequence of Job's encounter with Yahweh shows up in Ezekiel's vision. Now Jung says:

> The first great vision is made up of two well-ordered compound quaternities, that is, conceptions of totality, such as we frequently observe today as spontaneous phenomena. Their *quinta essentia* is represented by a figure which has the "likeness of a human form." (1:26).

Now here is Jung's unique contribution; who else would have interpreted it this way? He is talking about the fact that above the vault on that throne is a figure in the likeness of a man. So it's a human form. Jung says:

> Here Ezekiel has seen the essential content of the unconscious [as a consequence of Job's encounter], namely *the idea of the higher man* by whom Yahweh was morally defeated and who he was later to become. . . .
> Ezekiel grasped, in a symbol, the fact that Yahweh was drawing closer to man. This is something which came to Job as an experience but probably did not reach his consciousness. . . . What is more, in Ezekiel we meet for the first time the title "Son of Man," which Yahweh significantly uses in addressing the prophet, presumably to indicate that he is a son of the "Man" on the throne.[35]

That's Jung's interpretation of the man on the throne in Ezekiel's vision

Now I want to read you something from Gershom Scholem's *Major Trends in Jewish Mysticism*. He has a whole chapter on the Merkabah. Merkabah means "throne-chariot." You see, this vision of Ezekiel could be interpreted as a kind of chariot-throne—it involves a throne but the wheels also give it a chariot aspect. Scholem tells us that Ezekiel's vision of God's throne-chariot, the Merkabah, was a favorite subject of discussion and interpretation in Pharisaic circles which it was apparently inadvisable to make public. Originally these discussions were restricted to the elucidation and exposition of the respective Biblical passages, because there is a Jewish tradition which forbids the study of the beginning and the end of the Book of Ezekiel until you are thirty years old. The living crea-

---

[35] *Psychology and Religion*, CW 11, pars. 665f.

tures of Ezekiel's vision were conceived as angels who form a hierarchy at the Celestial Court. Those who devoted themselves to Merkabah mysticism gave a lot of attention to that imagery. Scholem writes:

> Not only had the seers perceived the celestial hosts, heaven with its angels, but the whole of a [certain group] of literature is shot through with a chain of new revelations concerning the hidden glory of the great Majesty, its throne, its palace . . . the celestial spheres, towering up one over the other, paradise, hell and the containers of the souls.[36]

All this goes to make up Merkabah mysticism, which has as its starting point this vision of Ezekiel.

Let us see how Jung has elaborated this symbolism. In *Aion* he starts with a Gnostic text, from which he derives a multiple image of the Self: four interconnected, three-dimensional tetrahedrons (below). You can study these at your leisure, from paragraph 328 of *Aion;* Jung's commentary on the Gnostic text, which is quite complex, starts with paragraph 359. Here I will speak a little more generally and a little more simply. You see, Jung condensed his vast experience of the various manifestations of

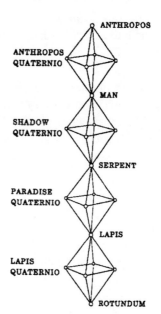

The structure of the Self.
(From Edinger, *The Aion Lectures,*
p. 179, bottom.)

---

[36] *Major Trends in Jewish Mysticism,* pp. 42f.

the Self into this chart. I want to try to make that available to you, at least enough so you will be able to think about it. It's not so easy to open up. It is obscure initially, but I will try.[37]

Think of those four tetrahedrons as four descending steps, starting with the very top term, the Anthropos. Now go through these four descending forms all the way down to the bottom, the Rotundum. These are sequential stages of embodiment of the Self, so to speak, as it descends from above. The top one is the Anthropos (or Spiritual) Quaternity. It is a human embodiment of the fourfold nature of the Anthropos, but in a higher or spiritual aspect. The next one, the Shadow Quaternity, is a manifestation of the quaternity of the Anthropos in a negative human aspect. The third one down, the Paradise Quaternity, has as its four terms the four rivers of Paradise, and it has garden or vegetation symbolism. So it's gone below the human and animal level, all the way down to plant imagery.

The fourth and lowest quaternity, which is made up of the four elements—air, fire, earth and water—belongs to matter. And that lowest quaternity has dropped all the way out of life entirely, and has reached the inorganic level. So what we have here, then, is a series of descending stages of manifestations of the Self from the most spiritual down to the human and then the lower human and animal, through to the vegetational, then finally down to the inorganic, the Lapis or Matter Quaternity.

Now having noticed that sequence, imagine it as a flexible cord or chain, as though these were beads on a cord, and imagine that the dot marked Rotundum at the very bottom is brought along up to the top and equated with the Anthropos. Then you've completed the circle. Then the uroborus has its tail in its mouth, and instead of a straight line you have a circle (opposite, top), which corresponds to the formulaic image in paragraph 410 of *Aion* (opposite, bottom).

I want to read you what Jung says about this formula, and then I'm going to try to open up at least a little bit what this means. So that you can begin to use it and to gather experience that will verify it for you. That is what I chiefly want to do. I hope to make it sufficiently available to you that you can start testing this formulation in your own experience or with patients' material.

---

[37] [For a more extensive commentary on these images, see Edinger, *The Aion Lectures: Exploring the Self in C.G. Jung's* Aion, chaps. 24-25.—Ed.]

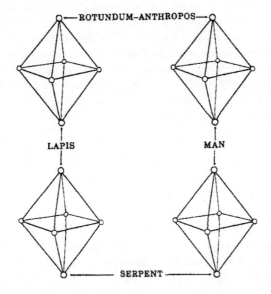

Formulaic images of the Self.
(Top, from Edinger, *The Aion Lectures,* p. 179;
bottom, from CW 9ii, p. 259.)

Jung says this:

> The "sublimation" or progress or qualitative change consists in an unfolding of totality into four parts four times, which means nothing less than its become conscious. When psychic contents are split up into four aspects, it means that they have been subjected to discrimination by the four orienting functions of consciousness. The process depicted by our formula changes the originally unconscious totality into a conscious one. The Anthropos A descends from above through his Shadow B into Physis [that is, nature] C (= serpent) [which is represented by a serpent or fish], and, through a kind of crystallization process D (= *lapis)* that reduces chaos to order, rises again to the original state, which in the meantime has been transformed from an unconscious into a conscious one.[38]

What he is saying here is that he is going through this fourfold cycle as a circle, instead of a downward line which is the way I went through it.

What these diagrams tell us, in very condensed form, is the fact that experiences and symbols of totality may manifest themselves on four different levels. So that there are really four different kinds of quaternities that one might come across in dealing with unconscious material. And I've labeled those four kinds the Spiritual Quaternity, the Shadow quaternity, the Paradise Quaternity, and the Matter Quaternity. Now let me say a few words about those and give you an example or two, because such images don't come to us with a label around their necks. One has to know them in advance. Otherwise, the distinction won't be made. There has to be a perceiving consciousness.

The Spiritual Quaternity will manifest in settings and in images that emphasize the heaven, the elevated, the ideal, airy, abstract kind of context. The Shadow Quaternity will manifest in dark and dubious human beings and/or animals. Jung tells us that what is called the lower Adam stands between the Spirit Quaternity and the Shadow Quaternity. The Paradise Quaternity, which is the third one, has as a kind of threshold guardian between it and the Shadow Quaternity—a serpent, or alternatively a fish. The Paradise Quaternity has vegetation or garden symbolism as its chief context, and the guardian or gateway between the Paradise Quaternity and the Matter Quaternity is the *lapis*—the stone. The Matter Quaternity has inorganic symbolism as its basis, usually stones or crystals

---

[38] *Aion,* CW 9ii, par. 410.

or geometrical forms, but nothing living. And, you see, an experience of wholeness can occur on each of these levels. If we're familiar with the different levels, then the particular experience of the particular image we're dealing with can be located.

Now I want to give you an example of the Heavenly or Spiritual mandala, which I take from Dante's *Paradiso*, canto 30. I'm passing around a picture of what I'm going to read (below):

The Empyrean, engraving by Gustav Doré, 1868.
(Photostatic transfer by Apple Press, Inc., Indianapolis.)

> There in Heaven, a lamp shines in whose light
> the Creator is made visible to His creature,
> whose one peace lies in having Him in sight.
>
> That lamp forms an enormous circle, such
> that its circumference, fitted to the Sun
> as a bright belt, would be too large by much.
>
> It is made up entirely of the reflection
> of rays that strike the top of the first-moved sphere,
> imparting to it all its power and motion.
>
> And as a slope shines in the looking glass
> of a lake below it, as if to see itself
> in its time of brightest flower and greenest grass;
>
> so, tier on tier, mounting within that light,
> there glowed, reflected in more than a thousand circles,
> all those who had won return to Heaven's height.
>
> And if so vast a nimbus can be bound
> within its lowest tier, what then must be
> the measure of this rose at its topmost round?[39]

It's a vision of a great heavenly rose, you see, of the elect, of the re-deemed. So they are human figures, but in a celestial, heavenly form.

> There, far and near cause neither loss nor gain,
> for where God rules directly, without agents,
> the laws that govern nature do not pertain.
>
> Into the gold of the rose that blooms eternal,
> rank on rank, in incenses of praise
> it sends up to the Sun forever vernal—[40]

That's an example of the Spiritual Quaternity. The others we will have to leave for another time.

---

[39] *The Divine Comedy,* lines 100-117.
[40] Ibid., lines 121-126.

6
Ezekiel, Part Two

Our assignment tonight is the second half of Ezekiel, which I will follow approximately but do a little free ranging, too. I'm going to talk about some of the themes that interest me, and also offer some further theoretical reflections on the relation between the ego and the Self that I think derive from our study of the prophets.

The Personal and the Collective

Previously, we noted several examples of how Ezekiel was ordered by Yahweh to act out symbolically, in his own personal life, the coming fate of Israel. For instance he was asked to act out the procedure of going into exile, by packing his bundle and taking off into the night. And he was asked to eat his food and drink his water in fear and trembling, in anticipation of the fact that all of Israel would be doing the same. So his personal life was to be an example or a symbol of the condition of the collective psyche. In chapter 24 Ezekiel provides us with another really quite terrible example of this same phenomenon:

> The word of Yahweh was addressed to me as follows, "Son of man, I am about to deprive you suddenly of the delight of your eyes [that means his wife]. But you are not to lament, not to weep, not to let your tears run down. Groan in silence. . . ." I told this to the people in the morning and my wife died in the evening, and the next morning I did as I had been ordered. . . . I replied [to them], "The word of Yahweh has been addressed to me as follows, 'Say to the House of Israel: The Lord Yahweh says this. I am about to profane my sanctuary, the pride of your strength, the delight of your eyes, the passion of your souls.' " (24:15-21)

So Ezekiel's loss of his wife who was the light of his eyes paralleled Israel's loss of the divine sanctuary which was the delight of the eyes of Israel.

Now to understand this psychologically I am inclined to reconstruct the sequence of events. I would hypothesize that the first thing that happened was that Ezekiel's wife died. And then in his grief, in his questioning of what that tragedy meant to him, Yahweh comes to him in active imagination or in a dream or some manifestation from the unconscious, and informs him that the death of his wife parallels Israel's fate of losing the delight of her eye—the sanctuary.

That's the way it happens in psychological experience. First one has the event, the crippling, agonizing event, and then in the process of trying to assimilate it, come to terms with it, one may discover its archetypal background—that there's a larger context to it, a more than personal meaning. And even though that does not eliminate the pain of the experience, it makes the pain meaningful. To discover the archetypal background is indeed healing, I think chiefly because with that discovery the ego is released from identification with an archetypal experience. What is so intolerably burdensome is to carry personally a weight of meaning that is transpersonal. When one can get out from under that excessive weight by the process of disidentification, then there's a sense of release.

In chapter 33 there's another theme that we've encountered earlier, and that's the idea that if the prophet does not warn the sinner to correct his evil ways, then the prophet carries the responsibility for the sinner's death. This comes up in a little different form in chapter 33 where the prophet is compared to a sentry who is on the lookout for danger to the city. And whenever he spies anything suspicious or potentially dangerous the sentry blows his trumpet to sound the warning. This is the same function that Yahweh requires of the prophet.

I think we can see something of an analogy to what the analyst must do when he sees psychological peril. For instance, we must warn patients when evidence in dreams suggests there's a dangerous proneness to accident. A classic example is Jung's account of being told, not even by a patient, just by an acquaintance, about a dream of walking off the edge of a mountain.[41] Jung warned him most earnestly not to go mountain climbing. The man ignored the warning and later died in a mountain climbing expedition. That's the sentry function of the analyst.

The Good Shepherd

In chapter 34 we have a very fine expression of an important archetypal image, that of the good shepherd. Yahweh is described as the good shepherd, in the midst of a promise to regather the scattered people of Israel:

---

[41] See "The Practical Use of Dream-Analysis," *The Practice of Psychotherapy,* CW 16, pars. 323f.

For the Lord Yahweh says this: I am going to look after my flock myself
and keep all of it in view. As a shepherd keeps all his flock in view when he
stand sup in the middle of his scattered sheep, so shall I keep my sheep in
view. I shall rescue them from wherever they have been scattered during the
mist and darkness. I shall bring them out of the countries where they are; I
shall gather them together from foreign countries and bring then back to
their own land. I shall pasture them on the mountains of Israel, in the ra-
vines and in every inhabited place in the land. I shall feed them in good
pasturage; the high mountains of Israel will be their grazing ground. There
they will rest in good grazing ground; they will browse in rich pastures on
the mountains of Israel. I myself will pasture my sheep, I myself will show
them where to rest—it is the Lord Yahweh who speaks. I shall look for the
lost one, bring back the stray, bandage the wounded and make the weak
strong. I shall watch over the fat and healthy. I shall be a true shepherd to
them. (34:11-16)

I think we have in that passage a beautiful example of the integrative,
consolidating aspect of the Self after a period of fragmentation and multiple dissociation represented by the scattering. Because what's being
promised here is that there will be consolidation, a unification of the scattered, separated fragments. And that is indeed something we observe happening, especially in times of severe psychic stress. Or when there is a
tendency to fragmentation such an experience seems also to constellate the
integrative aspect of the Self, the "good shepherd" aspect.

That's such an important image that I wanted to linger with it for a
while, to let it sink in.

The Hebrew word for shepherd is *ro'eh*, which comes from a very
similar verb *ra'ah* which means to pasture or to shepherd. So that the
noun, the function of shepherd, is basically a nourishing, pasturing function. That, of course, is also the source of the word "pastor" as used for the
ministerial function. To be a pastor means to provide pasture for the sheep
under one's care. The Church congregation is a sheepfold with a pastor.

This image first appears in the Old Testament in chapter 49 of Genesis,
verse 24. It isn't in the Jerusalem Bible; they used a different textual
authority, but it's in the Authorized Version. And in that verse Yahweh is
called "the shepherd" and "the stone" of Israel. And there are several other
important references to the image of Yahweh as a shepherd. One of the
most important is Psalm 23, which starts out with the phrase "Yahweh is
my shepherd." And Psalm 80 begins with the statement directed to Yah-

weh: "Shepherd of Israel, listen, you who lead Joseph like a flock." Then we have the important passage in Isaiah, which says,

> He is like is like a shepherd feeding his flock,
> gathering lambs in his arms,
> holding them against his breast
> and leading to their rest the mother ewes. (Isa. 40:11)

And then finally a passage in Jeremiah that reads,

> Listen, nations, to the word of Yahweh.
> Tell this to the distant islands,
> "He who scattered Israel gathers him,
> he guards him as a shepherd guards his flock." (Jer. 31:10)

Of course, this image of the good shepherd became a very important image in Christian symbolism. And the major text for that, as applied to Christ, is found in the Book of John, which I will read because it's such a fully rounded elaboration. This is Christ speaking:

> "I tell you most solemnly, anyone who does not enter the sheepfold through the gate, but gets in some other way is a thief and a brigand. The one who enters through the gate is the shepherd of the flock; the gatekeeper lets him in, the sheep hear his voice, one by one he calls his own sheep and leads them out. When he has brought out his flock, he goes ahead of them, and the sheep follow because they know his voice. They never follow a stranger but run away from him: they do not recognize the voice of strangers."
>
> . . . .
>
> Jesus spoke to them again:
> "I tell you most solemnly,
> I am the gate of the sheepfold.
> All others who have come
> are thieves and brigands;
> but the sheep took no notice of them.
> I am the gate.
> Anyone who enters through me will be safe:
> he will go in freely in and out
> and be sure of finding pasture.
> The thief comes
> only to steal and kill and destroy.
> I have come
> so that they may have life
> and have it to the full.
> I am the good shepherd:

the good shepherd is one who lays down his life for his sheep.
The hired man, since he is not the shepherd
and the sheep do not belong to him,
abandons the sheep and runs away
as soon as he sees a wolf coming,
and then the wolf attacks and scatters the sheep;
this is because he is only a hired man
and has no concern for the sheep.
I am the good shepherd;
I know my own
and my own know me,
just as the Father knows me
and I know the Father;
and I lay down my life for my sheep.
And there are other sheep I have
that are not of this fold,
and these I have to lead as well.
They too will listen to my voice,
and there will be only one flock,
and one shepherd." (John 10:1-16)

That's the Christian elaboration of the good shepherd archetype.

Now, it happens that Jung talks about this image in his *Visions Seminars*. In order to elaborate further I'm going to read you a little section from it. The patient Jung speaks about had, in one of her early dreams, a shepherd dream, as follows:

I was in a boat with some man. He said, "We must go to very end of the lake, where the four valleys converge, where they bring down the flocks of sheep to the water." When we got there, he found a lame sheep in the flock, and I found a little lamb that was pregnant. It surprised me because it seemed too young to be pregnant. We tenderly took those two sheep in our arms and carried them to the boat. I kept wrapping them up. The man said, "They may die, they are shivering so." So I wrapped them up once more. [42]

That's the dream.

I'm inclined to think that the majority of individual dreams that Jung chooses to report and interpret have a more than individual meaning; they can also be understood as having a general or collective validity. And I think so of this dream too.

These sheep, one of which is lame and one pregnant—this whole flock

---

[42] *The Visions Seminars*, vol. 1, p. 19.

that's in need of attention—could be thought of as referring to our collective need for relation to God, our need for shepherding guidance. In other words, our need for a recovery of a religious attitude that has been lost through the breakdown of the traditional religious container. One is lame and one is pregnant. In other words, the situation of the sheep is damaged on the one hand and is pregnant with future prospects on the other hand. So they are in need of healing and are also carrying potential new life. Those are some of my own general remarks on the dream.

But the reason I brought it up is that I want to read part of Jung's commentary on this dream, because it involves the theme of the good shepherd. It's also a good example of Jung's free-ranging amplification.

[In the dream we have] the figure of the shepherd who picks up a little lamb and carries it. You see here the man assumes the role of the good shepherd. Already, he is a guide—he guides the dreamer to the place of the four valleys and when he comes to his flock picks up a lame sheep. He is a figure that can be likened to a very interesting figure of the primitive church, called the *Poimen*, which has now vanished from ecclesiastical terminology. The good shepherd has remained, but the other figure has vanished with a certain book that was almost canonical at the time called *The Shepherd of Hermas*. When the New Testament writings were gathered together, that was omitted. I must use the Greek word *Poimen* here, because this *Poimen* is a pre-Christian figure. It is not a Christian invention, it is a pagan invention, and has a direct historical relation to Orpheus. And Orpheus is another figure related to Christ; he was understood to be an anticipation of Christ because he tamed wild passions in the form of wild animals by his delicate music. He is also like a shepherd, and moreover he is called "the Fisher," and as such he played a great role in the Dionysian mysteries which were of course pre-Christian. So we see the Christ figure in heathen cults. . . .

In very early times he was not a person at all, and so he was always handled in that way—symbolized accordingly. So for instance, the form of the *Poimen* was a sort of tremendous big angel, of more than human size, a great invisible spirit, a good God, and that very impersonal figure was never called Christ. That name was taboo. He was called the Shepherd of Men—Poimandres, the great leader of men, a mystery man, but directly related to *The Shepherd of Hermas*, which is decidedly Christian. . . . We have the pagan form in a very interesting Greek text, and the best idea I can give you of that is that it is a book which might have written by an analytic patient about his or her visions, about how the *Poimen* appeared to him or to her. It was a man who wrote it because the mysteries were then chiefly a man's business.

To-day they are a woman's business. In that text you find a description of how the *Poimen* appeared to him, what his teachings was, and how he received guidance through the *Poimen*, the leader or shepherd of men.

Now our good lady has of course not the least idea of what she is dreaming. It is just that unknown man who picks up the sheep, but you see as a matter of fact she returns here to the archetypal pattern really of the spirit-like leader of men. It goes right back to the spirit-leader of primitive tribes—where certain men called medicine men are at times possessed by spirits . . . who lead them and tell what is good for the people.[43]

He then goes on to give an example of Eskimos crossing the Bearing Straits through the inspiration of a medicine man.

Now I will read to you a passage from *The Shepherd of Hermas* that Jung refers to, to complete my amplification of this good shepherd image:

While I was praying at home and sitting on my bed, there entered a man glorious to look upon, in the dress of a shepherd, covered with a white goat-skin, with a bag on his shoulders and a staff in his hand. And he greeted me and I greeted him back. And at once he sat down by me, and said to me, "I have been sent by the most reverend angel to dwell with you the rest of the days of your life." I thought he was come tempting me, and said to him, "Yes, but who are you?" . . . He said to me, "Do you not recognize me?" "'No," I said. "I," said he, "am the shepherd to whom you were handed over." [That refers to some previous experience that we don't know about.] While he was still speaking,, his appearance changed, and I recognized him, that it was he to whom I was handed over; and at once I was confounded, and fear seized me, and I was quite overcome with sorrow that I had answered him so basely and foolishly. But he answered me and said, "Be not confounded, but be strong in my commandments which I am going to command you. For I was sent," said he, "to show you again all the things you saw before. . . . First of all write my commandments and the parables."[44]

This is followed by a very long sequence of instructions as to what he's to do. As Jung said, this sort of thing is quite analogous to what an analytic patient might do in active imagination. The shepherd is the guide of the sheeplike or helpless aspects of the psyche that must be in communication with the guiding, shepherding aspect of the Self. Otherwise he's a lost sheep who is hopelessly astray.

---

[43] Ibid., pp. 24f.

[44] *The Shepherd of Hermas*, vision 5, sect. 1-5, in *The Apostolic Fathers*, vol. 2, pp. 69ff.

Relations Between the Ego and the Self

In chapter 36 of the Book of Ezekiel, Yahweh states that he is going to gather together scattered Israel, and then proceeds to say:

> I am not doing this for your sake, House of Israel, but for the sake of my holy name. . . . I mean to display the holiness of my great name, which has been profaned among the nations, which you have profaned among them. (36:22-23)

What I want to draw your attention to is this explicit statement that what Yahweh does, He does for the sake of His holy name and not for the sake of Israel. We have other examples where that same point is made, for instance in Psalm 106:

> [Our ancestors] failed to appreciate your great love,
> they defied the Most High at the Sea of Reeds.
> For the sake of his name, he saved them
> to demonstrate his power. (106:7-8)

Then the most explicit of all is in Isaiah 48, where Yahweh says:

> And now I have put you in the fire like silver,
> I have tested you in the furnace of distress.
> for my sake and my sake only have I acted—
> is my name to be profaned?
> Never will I yield my glory to another. (48:10-11)

I think what this refers to psychologically is the fact that the Self sends both help and problems to the ego for the sake of the Self. In other words, I don't think one should have too sentimental or innocent an attitude about the nature of the Self. Like everything alive, everything in the biological world, the Self is concerned with survival and Self-realization. It is concerned with itself, and interested in the ego pretty much only for how the ego can serve it. The Self is just as Self-centered as the ego is ego-centered. In fact the ego is a kind of replica of the Self. And that's why we're so self-centered, self with a small letter, because we're a chip off the old block, you see. We're made of the same stuff. And these scriptures make that explicit.

As you know, throughout the course of these lectures, we've been considering all the Old Testament material as a record of the ego's relation to the Self. First of all, Yahweh's relation to Israel—Israel being thought of as a sort of collective ego—and then after Job's encounter a more individualized relationship seems to develop. Today I want to try to widen our exploration to some of the more marginal aspects of the ego and the Self, as the psychological data seem to suggest. What I'm going to offer is hypothetical; it's not fixed and fully established. It is one way to encourage exploratory thinking about how we can order certain data that are being accumulated as we gain more and more experience in depth psychology.

You will recall that Yahweh told Isaiah, Jeremiah and Ezekiel that he was using the Assyrians and the Babylonians to punish Israel for their sins. And we're told in many places that famine and plague and storms and earthquakes were also punishments from Yahweh. For example, in Isaiah 29 he says:

> Suddenly, unexpectedly,
> you shall be visited by Yahweh Sabaoth
> with thunder, earthquake, mighty din,
> hurricane, tempest, flame of devouring fire. (29:5)

So you see that both the military empires, the agencies of man, and the elements were described as operational instruments of Yahweh. Certainly the Assyrians and Babylonians were pursuing their own purposes. I have no doubt about that. They didn't think they were agents of Yahweh's divine vengeance, but the prophets stated that they were merely the instruments in Yahweh's relation to Israel.

Now when we try to grasp such statements psychologically, what we're reminded of is a certain kind of psychological phenomenon that is called "ideas of reference." This is a symptom of psychosis, a decompensation of the ego. An idea of reference refers to the feeling, to the impression or conviction that some objective phenomenon is personally related to my own psychology. If I'm watching television, for instance, and I see the news commentator grimacing, and I say, "Ah, he is trying to communicate a message to me," that is an idea of reference. And whatever the message is I spin it out. You see the television commentator doesn't have anything to do with me; he's an objective phenomenon. But if I project onto him some inner figure that is trying to convey a message to me, then I begin to have that delusional idea of reference.

Well, that is not too remote from the way the Hebrew prophets interpreted the invasions of Assyria and Babylonia when they said that they were coming in as part of the message from Yahweh to Israel. It's an idea of reference. A grand idea of reference.

However it's also true that external events, when one is open to a certain depth of the unconscious, can speak to one and refer to one's personal psychology through meaningful synchronistic phenomena. We know that to be a fact. And the only thing that distinguishes the experience of synchronicity from the psychotic's idea of reference is a well-developed ego. That's a pretty big distinction, but that's what it is. Anyhow, we've accumulated a fairly large body of experience in these matters, and I think the time has come to try to formulate hypotheses that will order this data and at least start to explain it.

We do have reason to believe that the actions of others and the actions of the objective, material world speak to the individual psyche. How can we hold onto that conviction without falling into a psychotic, solipsistic idea of reference? That's the question. We need some adequate image of how to understand these experiences.

My chart (opposite) is a feeble effort in that direction. What I'm trying to portray in it is some of the following: The universe is an organism, I mean by that a living organism, which is permeated throughout either with manifest or with latent life and psyche. And the individual human psyche would just be the most conscious flower of that organism, so to speak, of that particular garden. But the totality of this latently alive and psychic universe I would call "the cosmic Self." I would also postulate, although this is with more uncertainty—the data is not very strong yet for this—that there exists a center within the totality of that cosmic Self. And if there's a center then there's a functioning reactive agency within that cosmic totality. If that in fact exists, Yahweh, as he's described in the Old Testament, would be a symbolic image of that center, since he's described specifically as having universal attributes, of being both the creator and the master of the whole universe. That's the first principal of the hypothesis.

The second principle is that in this cosmic, psychic sea, individual psyches swim about like fish, carrying different degrees of consciousness. Now if we look at the diagram, the great circle that you see less than all of, the great arc, corresponds to what I mean by the cosmic Self. And I postulate that it has a center, which means it has a quasi-personality. Does it have consciousness? Well, I don't know. I don't even know whether the center exists, that's still a postulate.

I think of the arc of this circle as being of the phenomenal world. I indicate that in the label, where the Xs are. Those Xs are events, objects

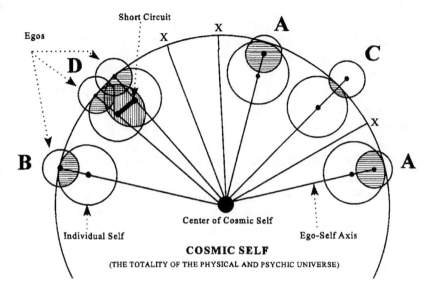

A: largely unconscious individuals in a state of participation mystique with the individual Self and the Cosmic Self

B: individuals on the verge of becoming conscious of the Self

C: an individuated individual aware of the Self and the ego-Self axis

D: two individuals in a state of mutual identity (the same set-up applies to group psychology)

X: inorganic matter and objective events on the circumference of the Cosmic Self; the totality of the physical and psychic universe, i.e., the world as phenomena

and events in the phenomenal world. And the various circles here indicate individuals—individual psychic entities. The smallest circles represent individual egos, the middle size circles represent the Self in its individual aspect, and the lines represent the connecting links between the ego and the individual Self, and between the individual Self and the center of the cosmic Self. And you will notice that I've also indicated that different individuals have different levels of consciousness. Some are more conscious than others, as is indicated by having a larger portion of the ego circle outside the arc of the cosmic Self.

Several things I would draw your attention to. One is the phenomenon of identity between the ego and the Self. There will be the most degree of ego-Self identity with those circles that are least developed, most unconscious. And ego-Self identity means that archetypal contents from the individual Self are personalized or ego-ized, so to speak, which would be a state of narcissistic inflation with infantile attitudes requiring a reductive approach.

A second area is that of individual selfhood, which is signified by the middle-sized circle. That area of individual selfhood would correspond to authentic, archetypal and transpersonal factors which belong chiefly to the individual. They belong to one's fate, one's individual myth, and even though they are collective in their nature they are individual in their manifestations. As one encounters those contents in the process of analysis, they require a synthetic approach, archetypal amplification, what I would call a personal synthetic approach. So that they would be interpreted along the lines of one's individual destiny or personal myth, or how one's personal myth relates to the archetypal image.

But then there is a third area that I represent in this chart, the area of collective or cosmic Selfhood. That's the area represented by this great circle with the major center, which would refer to the largest, most comprehensive cosmic and historical processes. And if an individual has an encounter with contents from that cosmic region, the cosmic Self, it would indicate—and be a highly unusual phenomenon—that one has a task as an instrument of cosmic evolution, a very extraordinary fate. This would call for a quite impersonal synthetic approach—not a personal synthetic approach—but an impersonal synthetic approach in which the chief concern would be for the transpersonal process and not for the individual.

I think that level of understanding and interpretation can only be conceived in terms of Jungian psychology, and the only reason it's available to Jungian psychology is because of Jung himself. He was such a person. He had an historical, cosmic destiny to fulfill, and therefore he encountered that level in his own psyche and therefore he built it in to his own psychological system. A person who did not have that in his own psyche could never have included it in his system. That's why we have such a comprehensive approach in analytical psychology.

Anyway, there are those three levels. And my hope is that this diagram can help to explain how certain experiences of the unconscious can come to us from the world and from other people. In other words, not just from our dreams and from the unconscious—from the inside—but also from the unconscious from the outside. This is always something that beginners in analysis have trouble with. It's difficult for them to see that the outer experience that happens to an individual can reflect that individual's psychology. The reason that's so hard is that a certain depth experience of the unconscious has to have been achieved before this fact becomes visible. Before then it doesn't exist and indeed it's a kind of a crazy idea. People look at you very strangely if you start talking that way. So you shouldn't talk that way to the wrong people.

What I purport to suggest in this chart is that each ego is in latent connection with all human beings, and, quite beyond that, with the whole world, with all that exists and happens. We get occasional glimpses of this fact in experiences of synchronicity.

It is also possible that other people's reactions to us may very well convey messages from the Self. In other words, other people can be Assyrians or Babylonians to our Israel. It's not always negative; there can also be positive Assyrians and Babylonians. But as this chart would suggest, and as I think a good bit of psychological data indicates, on certain levels of the unconscious everything is connected with everything else. Also, the individual Self is not distinguished from the collective Self, or is very imperfectly distinguished.

I think for example of a man I saw in the mental hospital many years ago, whose psychosis began when he started having delusions that he was receiving telepathic messages from people all over the country. And it finally became a fixed idea, that he was the communications center for the whole country, the central switchboard, through which everything was connected. In other words, he had fallen into an identification with the cosmic Self, not just the individual Self, but the cosmic Self.

Now, a special situation pertains in item D in the chart. This is the situation that occurs when there is an identification or a sizable psychic overlap between two individual psyches. This is the sort of phenomenon that takes place with major projections, falling in love or falling in hate or falling into some mutual archetypal dynamism that establishes a very sizable psychic overlap between the individual Self of the one person and the individual Self of the other person. When that happens, as I try to indicate provisionally in the diagram, one individual experiences connection with the Self through the other individual. It's as though one is cut off from one's own direct connection with the Self, and what I call a short circuit takes place. And in such a case, if one individual prematurely loses contact with the other, the break of the ego-Self connection can be so grave that they may not be able to survive. It can lead to the death or suicide of the grieving one, which is a danger in any strong transference situation.

This is a very crude, initial effort to reflect on these phenomena in as broad a context as possible. I offer it to you because I want to encourage you to start thinking, and because I think we need to start framing hypotheses of this sort.

7

Daniel; Hosea

Daniel

The Book of Daniel is psychologically very rich. It has a lot of symbolism in it, a lot of big images that are arresting and engaging, powerful dreams and visions. I shall only be able to deal briefly with some of the material.

Nebuchadnezzar's Two Dreams

Daniel starts right off with two dreams of Nebuchadnezzar: the dream of the statue and the dream of the tree. I think of those two dreams as belonging to a series, so I'll discuss them together. Let's imagine we're listening to a patient who has brought us these dreams. This is Daniel describing the first dream to Nebuchadnezzar:

> A great statue of extreme brightness stood before you, terrible to see. The head of this statue was of fine gold, its chest and arms were of silver, its belly and thighs of bronze, its legs of iron, its feet part iron, part earthenware. While you were gazing, a stone broke away, untouched by any hand, and struck the statue, struck its feet of iron and earthenware and shattered them. And then, iron and earthenware, bronze, silver, gold all broke into small pieces as fine as chaff on the threshing floor in summer. The wind blew them away, leaving not a trace behind. And the stone that had struck the statue grew into a great mountain, filling the whole earth. (2:31-35)

That was the first dream. Here is Nebuchadnezzar describing his second dream to Daniel, the tree dream:

> I saw a tree of great height at the center of the world. It was large and strong with its top touching the heavens, and it could be seen to the ends of the earth. Its leaves were beautiful and its fruit abundant, providing food for all. Under it the wild beasts found shade, in its branches the birds of the air nested; all men ate of it. In the vision I saw while in bed, a holy sentinel came down from heaven and cried out:
>
>> "Cut down the tree and lop off its branches,
>>> strip off its leaves and scatter its fruit;
>>> let the beasts flee its shade, and the birds its branches.
>> But leave in the earth its stump and roots,

fettered with iron and bronze, in the grass of the field.
Let him be bathed with the dew of heaven;
his lot be to eat, among beasts, the grass of the earth.
Let his mind be changed from the human;
let him be given the sense of a beast
till seven years pass over him.
By decree of the sentinels [or watchers] is this decided,
by order of the holy ones, this sentence;
That all who live may know
that the Most High rules over the kingdom of men:
He can give it to whom he will,
or set over it the lowliest of men." (4:7-14, NAB)

Now, what would we say if a patient brought us such a dream series? I think what I would say is that you are in great danger because you are identified with the Self. I would consider both statue and tree images as Self images that are in the process of being superseded. It is a help to have both these dreams together. We might interpret the tree dream a little differently just by itself. But if you have it in conjunction with the statue dream, that gives you a better sense of what to emphasize. Because it is a kind of tree of life dream. Of course it is the great central tree, too, but along with the dream of the statue it indicates that one particular embodiment or manifestation or expression of the Self is in the process of being destroyed and superseded.

Now let's take each of them separately.

In the first dream, the statue is a composite of the four metals plus a fifth element, clay. Statues, we know, are Self images; you can read about that in *Mysterium Coniunctionis*,[45] but this statue is a kind of patchwork, a composite that's put together, not an organic unity. It is a kind of contrived or artificial unit. This is what undergoes destruction, and what destroys it is a stone, a stone that "broke away, untouched by any hand," in other words, a stone with autonomous force within itself. So it would signify a more authentic, autonomous emergent Self that broke away of its own power. It would correspond, I think, to Yahweh as a rock or the stone that the builder's rejected or the Philosophers' Stone of the alchemists. Anyway the stone, the autonomous stone, becomes the replacement for the

---

[45] CW 14, pars. 559f; see also Edinger, *The Mysterium Lectures: A Journey Through Jung's* Mysterium Coniunctionis, pp. 234ff.

composite patchwork statue.

The tree dream has a little different emphasis. This is not an uncommon type of dream. I think I've had occasion to mention it before, the image of felling a very large and important tree. It indicates the dissolution or breakup of a major organic libido container on the vegetative level. Since it's a tree, it's on the plant level and that indicates a quantity of libido on the vegetative level. It generally refers to the breakup of a major personal relationship that has a very large component of unconscious identity attached to it, or the breakup of a connection to a collectivity: the church or an institution of some kind that has been a container for unconscious vegetative libido.

Here my hunch is that Nebuchadnezzar's dream signifies the loss of a condition of *participation mystique* with his kingdom, because the tree is described in the nature of a kingdom—a great collective entity. That's also indicated by what happens to the dreamer when the tree comes down: he's thrown out of his containment, out of his psychological cradle, you might say; he's thrown into temporary insanity, grazing on grass like the beasts in the field. He loses his reason temporarily, at least for seven years.

The Fiery Furnace

An important image in the Book of Daniel is the story of the three Hebrews in the fiery furnace. I see this story as a symbolic link to the dream of the broken statue, by virtue of the fact that the story also contains an image of a statue. It starts by Nebuchadnezzar's erecting a golden statue and decreeing that it be worshipped. The three Hebrews who refused to worship the statue correspond in their functioning to the stone that destroyed the statue in the dream, because Nebuchadnezzar was reduced to a helpless ravening beast by their refusal. But let me go through the story first, as told in chapter 3.

The story is that Nebuchadnezzar erected this golden statue and required that all bow down and worship it. And those who would not do so were to be punished by being thrown into a fiery furnace. The three pious Hebrews—Shadrach, Meshach and Abednego—refused to worship the king's statue. This enraged the king and they were thrown into the furnace. But they remain unharmed, and in addition to their walking about in the midst of the flames, a fourth figure is also seen in the flames, one who is said to look like a son of the gods, namely an angel.

I see this story as symbolizing the process of challenging arbitrary authority, arbitrary because it is based on the personal power motive. This challenge can be administered either to an outer arbitrary authority or to an inner one. In other words, one's own inner power motive.

Arbitrary authority is based on an inflated identification with the ego, and the person so caught behaves as though he or she is a deity. And such a condition can only be successfully challenged from within an authentic, conscious relation to the Self. It's the only way one can get away with challenging such authority. The three Hebrews had that prerequisite, because through their worship of Yahweh they each had an individual connection to the Self, and therefore could dare to disobey the king. That connection makes them immune to Nebuchadnezzar's wrath—which is represented by the fiery furnace.

To my mind, the wrath and the fiery furnace are two manifestations of the same phenomenon. And, of course, it's a *calcinatio* image. The *calcinatio* process burns away whatever is flimsy and not solidly based, leaving only the imperishable residue. These three Hebrews are of that nature; they're imperishable by virtue of their connection to the Self. They meet the test in the fire because they are already refined. The fact that they are unharmed means that they are the pure stuff, so to speak. This would refer psychologically to the ability to endure intense affect, either one's own affect from within or some intense affect from without, the frustrated arbitrary authority, Nebuchadnezzar in this case. To be able to endure such an affect without being consumed by it means to be able to encounter it without becoming possessed by it, without having the fire spread to oneself, so to speak. This relative immunity is generally created through a connection with the Self.

I think the same idea is expressed in the story in chapter 6 concerning Daniel in the lion's den. In that case it's a matter of being in such a relationship to the masculine instincts, signified by the lion, that one is not in danger of being eaten up by them, which means possessed by them, with the accompanying loss of ego consciousness.

Handwriting on the Wall

Another symbolically interesting story is in chapter 5, where during Belshazzar's feast a hand appears and writes on the wall. This, of course, has become built into the whole collective as a kind of proverbial image— the handwriting on the wall, the universal expression of the manifestation of destiny: what's coming, what's in store. What does the hand write? It writes, *"Mene, Mene, Teqel* and *Parsin."*

Now as one explores these terms a little bit, we learn—and a footnote in the Jerusalem Bible alludes to this fact—that what Daniel extracts from his words is not their exact meaning. He makes what you might call a kind of creative interpretation of these words, because they don't mean exactly what they say. In fact, nobody is absolutely certain what they do mean.

I want to consider them, first of all, just in terms of being four unknown words, two of which are a repetition of one, and then two others being separate. A note in some texts says there are only three words, the *Mene* is not repeated. In other words, we have the archetypal pattern here of three and maybe four. This hovering between three and four, which Jung has pointed out at length,[46] is an aspect of individuation imagery. The fourth term that completes the quaternity always comes reluctantly or ambiguously, and uncertainly; it's never thoroughly present. So here we have three terms, then a fourth term which is a repetition of the first.

We find the same phenomenon in the Tetragrammaton, which is composed of the four letters *jod, he, waw, he;* those are four terms but there are only three letters, because the *he* is repeated. So again there is this ambiguity between the three and the four. And you get it once again in what I would call the New Testament version of the Tetragrammaton—all the medieval pictures of the crucifixion, the sign that was hung on the cross, *Iesus Nazarenus Rex Iudaeorum, INRI,* Jesus of Nazareth, King of the Jews. But there again *INRI* is four letters but one of them repeats itself, the same as with the Tetragrammaton.

All these are examples of the quaternarian manifestation of the Self, with this ambiguous uncertainty as to whether three is going to be able to turn into four or not. That's what shows up in the handwriting on the wall, a manifestation of the Self. What Daniel then extracts in more specific terms from that manifestation are the terms "measured, weighed and divided." By sound familiarity he can reach those terms, "measured, weighed and divided," so his creative process then turns that into: "You've been measured, weighed in the balance and found wanting, and therefore your kingdom will be divided." So in this case the encounter with the Self, the handwriting on the wall, had the consequence of a *separatio* process:

---

[46] "A Psychological Approach to the Dogma of the Trinity," *Psychology and Religion,* CW 11, pars. 222ff.

measuring, weighing and division means that the ego is in the process of being separated from the Self.[47]

Daniel's Apocalyptic Vision

Chapter 7, which I consider the core of the Book of Daniel, has the major apocalyptic vision. This vision, together with some of the other visions that go to make up the Book of Daniel, constitutes really the original classic example of a whole genre of scriptural literature called "apocalyptic." This vision is really the first apocalypse. Daniel speaks:

> I saw that the four winds of heaven were stirring up the great sea; four great beasts emerged from the sea, each different from the other. The first was like a lion with eagle's wings; and as I looked its wings were torn off, and it was lifted from the ground and set standing on its feet like a man; and it was given a human heart. The second beast I saw was different, like a bear, raised up on one of its sides, with three ribs in its mouth. . . . "Up!" came the command. "Eat quantities of flesh!" After this I looked, and saw another beast, like a leopard, and with four birds' wings on its flanks; it had four heads, and power was given to it. Next I saw another vision . . . : a fourth beast, fearful, terrifying, very strong; . . . great iron teeth, and it ate, crushed and trampled underfoot what remained. It . . . had ten horns.
>
> While I was looking at these horns, I saw another horn sprouting among them, a little one, three of the original horns were pulled out by the roots to make way for it; and in this horn I saw eyes like human eyes, and a mouth that was full of boasts. As I watched:
>
>> Thrones were set in place
>> and one of great age took his seat.
>> [This is the so-called "Ancient of Days"]
>> His robe was white as snow,
>> the hair of his head as pure as wool.
>> His throne was a blaze of flames,
>> its wheels were a burning fire.
>> A stream of fire poured out,
>> issued from his presence.
>> A thousand thousand waited on him,
>> ten thousand times ten thousand stood before him.
>> A court was held
>> and the books were opened.

---

[47] [For a lengthy discussion of the *separatio* process, see Edinger, *Anatomy of the Psyche,* chap. 7.—Ed.]

The great things the horn was saying were still ringing in my ears, and as I watched, the beast was killed, and its body destroyed and committed to the flames. the other beasts were deprived of their power, but received a lease of life for a season and a time.

> I gazed into the visions of the night.
> And I saw, coming on the clouds of heaven,
> one like a son of man.
> He came to the one of great age
> and was led into his presence.
> On him was conferred sovereignty,
> glory and kingship,
> and men of all peoples, nations and languages became his servants.
> His sovereignty is an eternal sovereignty
> which shall never pass away,
> now will his empire ever be destroyed. (7:2-14)

I wanted to read that whole thing because it's such an important image in the history of apocalyptic visions.

The so-called apocalypses or revelations refer to eschatology. *Eschaton* in Greek means "last." It refers to the last things. This is a major theme in the New Testament too, especially in the Book of Revelation. It is also important to New Testament scholars, who question how much eschatological consciousness Christ had—the whole matter of the *parousia*, the Second Coming. Did Christ literally expect that to happen? It's a very sizable issue, and that means then there's an archetype of considerable importance at the bottom of it.

That's what I want to draw your attention to: how should we understand psychologically the whole issue of eschatology of these apocalyptic prophecies? I'll tell you how I understand it.

I understand eschatology psychologically as being an expression of the anticipated encounter with the activated Self projected into history. So the encounter with the Self enters into some future historical time. Now I do not mean to suggest by that interpretation that such a way of seeing would rule out an historical manifestation of such matters, because certainly synchronistic phenomena teach us that inner archetypal events can also occur externally. But considered psychologically, the historical manifestation would be secondary, and the psychological would be primary.

I've often thought, for instance, of passages in the Gospels where Christ says, in effect, "Many of you shall not die before you see the Son of

Man coming in glory."[48] Scholars generally interpret that to mean that
Christ literally expected the *parousia* or the Second Coming to occur
within the generation of the people he was speaking to. But it could just as
well be interpreted as meaning that some of them would have developed
psychologically sufficiently to experience that phenomenon internally.

These are just some of the ideas that come to mind when I think about
how to understand apocalyptic literature. But now let us look briefly at the
content of Daniel's vision as it might be interpreted psychologically and
not projected into history, which of course is what Daniel does. He interprets his vision as referring to successive kingdoms in history. But if we
avoid that historicizing of it and think of it psychologically, how would we
interpret such a vision? Well, here's how I see it.

It starts with four awesome beasts emerging from the ocean. There is a
Doré woodcut of it (opposite). I would see that as the primordial aspect of
the quaternity coming into view. It's Yahweh as beast, analogous to Behemoth and Leviathan which—as it emerges and comes into conscious
realization—calls up the requirement that it be tamed, transformed and
differentiated. And that indeed is what happens in the second part of the
vision. Because once the beast has arisen and one has this consciousness
of its fearful primitivity, then comes the image of the old man, the Ancient
of Days, sitting in his celestial court, a divine judgment scene, and the Son
of Man arriving in a cloud and being invested with sovereignty. Simultaneously with that, the beasts are either killed or subdued: one of them is
killed and the others are subdued.

Now one of the important features of the latter part of this vision is the
term Son of Man. You know Christ specifically applied this passage, this
particular vision in Daniel, to himself. When he was arrested and brought
before the Sanhedrin, he was asked by the High Priest,

> "Are you the Christ . . . the son of the Blessed One?" "I am," said Jesus,
> "and you will see the Son of Man seated at the right hand of the Power and
> coming with the clouds of heaven." (Mark 14:61-62)

Christ's reply is right out of Daniel 7:13; it's a quote from this particular
vision, applying to the Son of Man specifically.

---

[48] ["I tell you solemnly, there are some of these standing here who will not taste
death before they see the Son of Man coming with his kingdom." (Matt. 16:28; see
also Mark 9:1, Luke 9:27)—Ed.]

The Vision of the Four Beasts, engraving by Gustav Doré, 1865.
(Photostatic transfer by Apple Press, Inc., Indianapolis.)

Now, you'll remember that we first encountered this term, the Son of Man, in Ezekiel's vision in the first chapter of Ezekiel. You may also recall that Jung said Yahweh applied it to Ezekiel presumably to indicate that the son of the "Man" occupied the throne above the chariot, in other words was the deity in human manifestation.[49] What this all adds up to, as I understand it psychologically, is that the primordial Self, the primitive, unregenerate quaternity represented by the four beasts, undergoes transformation in the course of this vision whereby it is replaced or transformed by a new manifestation of the Self, the Messiah, called the Son of Man.

---

[49] See above, p. 82.

That title tells us what his essential nature is and what the nature of the transformation is. Since he's called the Son of Man, it means that the Self, the primordial Self, has undergone transformation by being humanized.

That's how I understand Daniel's vision, that Yahweh has been humanized from his bestial form.

Hosea

There is one really central theme or image in Hosea, especially if you look at it psychologically. That's the image of Yahweh's relation to Israel as a *coniunctio,* as a marriage. In line with this I would draw your attention to a paper by Rivkah Kluger, "The Image of the Marriage Between God and Israel in the Old Testament." Of course, this isn't the first time we've encountered this image, but somehow it takes on an explicitness in Hosea.

The Unfaithful Wife

The idea was that when Yahweh made his covenant with Israel, he married her, and Israel became his wife. But she was unfaithful to her marriage covenant; she became a whore. And worse yet, as elaborated in Hosea, the dowry given to her by her husband, Yahweh, was the very material she used to attract other lovers. This is stated explicitly in Ezekiel, where Yahweh says,

> You have taken my presents of gold and silver jewelry and made yourself human images to use in your whorings. . . . The bread I gave you, the finest flower, oil and honey which I used to feed you, you have now offered to them [the other lovers] as an appeasing fragrance [to the other gods]. (16:17-19)

Well, now this comes up in Hosea in these words:

> Denounce your mother, denounce her,
> for she is not my wife
> nor am I her husband.
> Let her rid her face of her whoring
> and her breasts of her adultery,
> or else I will strip her naked,
> expose her as on the day she was born;
> I will make a wilderness of her,
> turn her into an arid land,
> and leave her to die of thirst.
> I will not love her children,

since they are the children of whoring.
Yes, their mother has played the whore,
she who conceived them has disgraced herself.
"I am going to court my lovers," she said
"who give me my bread and water,
my wool, my flax, my oil and my drink."
She would not acknowledge, not she,
that I was the one who was giving her
the corn, the wine, the oil,
and who freely gave her that silver and gold
of which they have made Baals.
. . . .

I mean to make her pay for all the days
when she burned offerings to the Baals
and decked herself with rings and necklaces
to court her lovers,
forgetting me.
It is Yahweh who is speaking. (2:4-15)

That is absolutely explicit marriage symbolism, and as you know, it is duplicated in Christian imagery with the idea that the Church is the bride of Christ. We might also make the observation that like Israel, the Church has also played the harlot and used Christ's dowery for adulterous purposes. And as Yahweh turned against Israel, so God has abandoned his Church currently. I'd say a manifestation of this is Jung's childhood vision of God shitting on the roof of Basel Cathedral.[50] That is a supreme image of abandonment.

But to get back to the previous point. Israel supports her adulteries with the gifts of her husband Yahweh. Now what would that mean psychologically? It might mean that the ego takes the gifts of the Self and uses them for secular or idolatrous purposes. Somehow the transpersonal energy is misapplied for personal ends. Certainly, this is almost an inevitable aspect of ego development. The ego can't develop at all unless it does steal energy from the gods, from the archetypes, and use it for its own purposes. Nevertheless, sooner or later a time of reckoning comes; then the ego has to pay for that hubris. A kind of forced emptying of the ego takes place, represented here by Yahweh saying to Israel that he will withdraw all his gifts and strip her naked. That would correspond to the time when the ego must be stripped and emptied of all its stolen energies.

---

[50] *Memories, Dreams, Reflections,* pp. 39ff.

Then Yahweh goes on to say,

> That is why I am going to lure her
> and lead her out into the wilderness [after he has stripped her naked]
> and speak to her heart,
> I'm going to give her back her vineyards,
> . . . .
> [Then] she will respond to me as she did when she was young. (2:16-17)

So we have here the image of the wilderness as the place where the final emptying occurs, followed by a renewed filling, a renewed connection with the Self. Because after Israel has been stripped and emptied and lured out into the wilderness, then she's given back her vineyards.

Those quotations were a sort of background for the central story, which concerns Hosea's marriage. Yahweh comes to Hosea and says to him,

> Go, marry a whore, and get children with a whore, for the country itself has become nothing but a whore by abandoning Yahweh. (1:2)

Now, what does this mean? Hosea is asked to duplicate Yahweh's experience in his personal life. Yahweh has a whore for a wife. That's already established. So now Yahweh tells Hosea, since I have a whore for a wife, you have to go and take a whore for a wife too. In other words Hosea is asked to take on Yahweh's problem.

If we approach this psychologically, I imagine that it happened rather differently. I imagine that actually Hosea had an unfaithful wife, and in his anguish prayed to understand why this misfortune should happen to him. Perhaps he did active imagination, and did in fact contact Yahweh, who replied, in effect, "What are you complaining about? You're no worse off than I am. I've got a whore for a wife too." This is what we call discovering the archetypal meaning of the complex. And the consequence of it, Hosea's discovery that his burden is God's burden, is obviously going to change his whole attitude toward what's happened to him. It puts it in whole new context. It gives it a depth and breadth of meaning that it didn't have before, because what dawns on him then is that his personal problem makes him a carrier of a divine complex, we might say. And to the extent that he can endure his problem, or even resolve it, by becoming more conscious, he's contributing to the resolution of the divine complex.

You may have noticed that Jung mentions Hosea quite often, scattered throughout his work, which indicates that he felt a kinship with Hosea—I think in the sense of also being the carrier of a divine burden.

The Death of God

A modern example of the Hosea experience shows up in Nietzsche, who wrote the following in *The Gay Science:*

Have you not heard of that madman who lit a lantern in the bright morning hours, ran to the market place, and cried incessantly, "I seek God! I seek God!" As many of those who do not believe in God were standing around just then, he provoked much laughter. Why, did he get lost? said one? Did he lose his way like a child? said another. Or is he hiding? Is he afraid of us? Has he gone on a voyage? or emigrated? Thus they yelled and laughed. The madman jumped into their midst and pierced them with his glances.

"Wither is God?" he cried. "I shall tell you. We *have killed him*—you and I. All of us are his murderers. But how have we done this? How were we able to drink up the sea? Who gave us the sponge to wipe away the entire horizon? What did we do when we unchained this earth from its sun? . . . How shall we, the murderers of all murderers, comfort ourselves? What was holiest and most powerful of all that the world has yet owned has bled to death under our knives. Who will wipe this blood off us? . . ."

[Finally] the madman fell silent and . . . [his listeners] too were silent and stared at him in astonishment. At last he threw his lantern on the ground, and it broke and went out. "I come too early," he said then; "my time has not come yet. This tremendous event is still on its way, still wandering—it has not yet reached the ears of man. Lightning and thunder require time, the light of the stars requires time, deeds require time even after they are done, before they can be seen and heard. This deed is still more distant from them than the most distant stars—*and yet they have done it themselves.*"[51]

Walter Kaufmann says this about this passage:

Nietzsche prophetically envisages himself as a madman: to have lost God means madness; and when mankind will discover that it has lost God, universal madness will break out. This apocalyptic sense of dreadful things to come hangs over Nietzsche's thinking like a thundercloud

We have destroyed our own faith in God. There remains only the void. We are falling. Our dignity is gone. Our values are lost. . . . It has become colder, and night is closing in. Without seeking to explain away Nietzsche's illness, one can hardly fail today to consider it also symbolical. . . . We cannot distinguish what sense he may have had of his own doom from his presentiment of universal disaster.

---

[51] In Walter Kaufmann, trans. and ed., *The Portable Nietzsche*, pp. 95f.

The prophet Hosea was married, and when his wife became unfaithful to him, he experienced his relationship to her as a simile of God's relationship to Israel. Was not his wife as faithless as his people? Yet he loved her as God must love his people. Who can say if his anguished outcries, his protestations of his love, and his pleading for the loved one to return are meant for his wife or his people? Sometimes prophecy seems to consist in man's ability to experience his own wretched fate so deeply that it becomes a symbol of something larger. It is in this sense that one can compare Nietzsche with the ancient prophets. He felt the agony, the suffering, and the misery of a godless world so intensely, at a time when others were yet blind to its tremendous consequence, that he was able to experience in advance, as it were, the fate of a coming generation.[52]

I think that's a very interesting commentary from a philosopher, and we can arrive at a very similar idea by the psychological approach: Nietzsche indeed was living out a kind of symbolic life in an anticipation of what was to come.

The connection between Nietzsche and Hosea is relevant in another way too. In Hosea 6:6, Yahweh says:

What I want is love, not sacrifice;
knowledge of God, not holocausts.

I think this corresponds to Nietzsche's notion of what he called *amor fati*, love of fate. He puts it very succinctly in chapter two of his book, *Ecce Homo*, where he says:

My formula for greatness in a human being is *amor fati:* that one want nothing to be different—not forward, not backward, not in all eternity. Not merely bear what is necessary, still less conceal it . . . but *love* it.[53]

Of course, this has Nietzsche's characteristic inflated flavor to it. But nonetheless it's a very valid idea. And I think Jung describes a more modest version of this same thing: *amor fati* as the love-of-God attitude. Here is how Jung describes the way he was altered by his 1944 illness:

Something else, too, came to me from my illness. I might formulate it as an affirmation of things as they are: an unconditional "yes" to that which is, without subjective protests—acceptance of the conditions of existence as I see them and understand them, acceptance of my own nature, as I happen to be. . . .

---

[52] *Nietzsche: Philosopher, Psychologist, Antichrist,* pp. 97f.
[53] Ibid., p. 283.

It was only after the illness that I understood how important it is to affirm one's own destiny. In this way we forge an ego that does not break down when incomprehensible things happen; an ego that endures, that endures the truth, and that is capable of coping with the world and with fate. Then, to experience defeat is also to experience victory. Nothing is disturbed—neither inwardly nor outwardly, for one's own continuity has withstood the current of life and of time. But that can come to pass only when one does not meddle inquisitively with the workings of fate.[54]

This would correspond to *amor fati* and it would also correspond to love of God, which is what Yahweh tells Hosea he wants: love, love and knowledge of God; and love and knowledge are approximately equivalent in Old Testament terminology.

Let me give you one final thought that comes to me as I reflect on the story of Hosea. First Hosea is told to marry a whore, and thereby share Yahweh's fate of having the whore Israel as his wife. But then in chapter 3 Hosea is additionally told to love his whore wife and to take her back, "just as Yahweh gives his love to the sons of Israel though they turn to other gods." (3:1) I think if one reflects on the psychological implications of this story an implicit idea emerges, which is this. If Hosea can love his unfaithful wife, that will perhaps help Yahweh to recover His love for His own unfaithful wife, Israel. In other words, it's just possible that action of the human ego, Hosea in this case, is necessary to help bring about a new attitude in God.

That thought reminds me of a statement by Jung in his important letter to Elenid Kotschnig, where he says:

God can be called good only inasmuch as He is able to manifest His goodness in individuals. His moral quality depends upon individuals. That is why He incarnates. Individuation and individual existence are indispensable for the transformation of God the Creator.[55]

[54] *Memories, Dreams, Reflections,* p. 297.

[55] *Letters,* vol. 2, p. 314.

8
Jonah

The Book of Jonah is really a psychological gem. It's so concise and so meaningful that I'm going to go through it in its entirety and offer comments as I proceed.

The Flight from God

Jonah was a prophet of the eighth century B.C., during the reign of Jeroboam II. His name means "Dove." I am going to start right in at the beginning:

> The word of Yahweh was addressed to Jonah son of Amittai: "Up!" he said, "Go to Nineveh, the great city, and inform them that their wickedness has become known to me." Jonah decided to run away from Yahweh, and to go to Tarshish. He went down to Joppa and found a ship bound for Tarshish; he paid his fare and went aboard, to go with them to Tarshish, to get away from Yahweh. (1:1-3)

Yahweh is the activated Self who is calling Jonah, the ego, to give him an assignment; in other words He is calling him to the task of individuation. But the Jonah ego flees from the call of the Self. This theme, which is probably more explicit in Jonah than anywhere else in our mythological material, the theme of the flight from God, or the flight from the call to individuation, is very important psychologically because we encounter it so frequently in our work. It comes up in dreams all the time: flight dreams are very common. Often it is a flight from a shadow figure, but in some dreams it is explicitly a flight from the Self, as indicated by the imagery. I think we can say that almost always, behind flight dreams there is flight from the Self. Because if you are fleeing from the shadow, then you are fleeing from what stands behind it, which is the whole developmental process.

Whenever I think of Jonah's flight from God I think of the poet Francis Thompson and the classical expression he has given this theme of the flight from God in his poem, "The Hound of Heaven." I am going to read you a large section of that because I think it is so relevant to our work. But first let me say a few words about the personal life of Francis Thompson, for he really is or was a modern example of the Jonah experience.

Thompson lived from 1859-1907, dying of tuberculosis at the age of forty-eight. He was born in Preston, England, which is in the western section of England, close to Liverpool. He was a dreamy, introverted, inept youth. His father was a physician and wanted him to be a doctor. He meekly obliged his father by dutifully putting in six years at medical school, but flunking consistently—and finally giving it up. Somewhere about then he picked up an addiction to laudanum. He then spent about two more years living in the family home, drifting about, doing meaningless odd jobs. He was really fleeing from life during all that period.

Finally, like Jonah, he committed himself to the sea by leaving his parents' home and going to London, though he had nothing there to go to, actually. He just dove into the sea of London life, where he lived in a state of desperate vagrancy. He was on the edge of starvation a number of times, and almost died. At one time he was befriended by a prostitute. He reached the absolute bottom of existence. He did start to do a little writing and sent something to the editor of a literary magazine. From that this editor started assisting him, and with this help he recovered from his desperate state.

During his period of vagrancy and despair on the London streets Thompson must have had certain numinous experiences, because they show up in his later poetry. A particularly striking example are these last lines from "In No Strange Land (The Kingdom of God Is Within You)":

> But (when so sad thou canst not sadder)
> Cry—and upon thy so sore loss
> Shall shine the traffic of Jacob's ladder
> Pitched betwixt heaven and Charing Cross.[56]

Thompson surely descended into the belly of the whale during his three years of starving vagrancy, and he was rescued to fulfill his prophetic task of being a poet. I understand the personal level, at least, of "The Hound of Heaven" as deriving from that experience, from his attempt to escape life—both through drugs and through idleness—and also perhaps to escape his destined vocation as a poet. But as the poem emerges it takes on universal validity. I will read you the major portion of it, as an example of the first part of a modern Jonah experience: the part of fleeing from God.

---

[56] In Louis Untermeyer, ed., *A Concise Treasury of Great Poems,* p. 391.

I fled Him, down the nights and down the days;
  I fled Him, down the arches of the years;
I fled Him, down the labyrinthine ways
    Of my own mind; and in the mist of tears
I hid from Him, and under running laughter.
        Up vistaed hopes I sped;
        And shot, precipitated,
Adown Titanic glooms of chasmed fears,
  From those strong Feet that followed, followed after.
      But with unhurrying chase,
      And unperturbéd pace,
    Deliberate speed, majestic instancy,
      They beat—and a Voice beat
      More instant than the Feet—
    "All things betray thee, who betrayest Me."
      I pleaded, outlaw-wise,
By many a hearted casement, curtained red,
  Trellised with intertwining charities
(For, though I knew His love Who followéd,
      Yet was I sore adread
Lest, having Him, I must have naught beside);
But, if one little casement parted wide,
    The gust of His approach would clash it to:
    Fear wist not to evade, as Love wist to pursue.
Across the margent of the world I fled,
    And troubled the gold gateways of the stars,
    Smiting for shelter on their clanged bars;
      Fretted to dulcet jars
And silvern chatter the pale ports o' the moon.
I said to Dawn: Be sudden—to Eve: Be soon;
  With thy young skiey blossoms heap me over
    From this tremendous Lover—
Float thy vague veil about me, lest He see!

      . . . .
    Still with unhurrying chase,
    And unperturbéd pace,
  Deliberate speed, majestic instancy,
      Came on the following Feet,
      And a Voice above their beat—
"Naught shelters thee, who wilt not shelter Me."

He tries various other ways of escape. He seeks escape in children, in nature, in the weather. But always comes the voice that says,

    "Lo! naught contents thee, who content'st not Me."

Naked I wait Thy love's uplifted stroke!
My harness piece by piece Thou hast hewn from me,
  And smitten me to my knee;
  I am defenceless utterly.
  I slept, methinks, and woke,
And, slowly gazing, find me stripped in sleep.
In the rash lustihead of my young powers,
  I shook the pillaring hours
And pulled my life upon me; grimed with smears,
I stand amid the dust o' the mounded years—
My mangled youth lies dead beneath the heap.
My days have crackled and gone up in smoke,
Have puffed and burst as sun-starts on a stream.
  Yea, faileth now even dream
The dreamer, and the lute the lutanist;
Even the linked fantasies, in whose blossomy twist
I swung the earth a trinket at my wrist,
Are yielding; cords of all too weak account
For earth with heavy griefs so overplused.
  Ah! is Thy love indeed
A weed, albeit an amaranthine weed,
Suffering no flowers except its own to mount?
  Ah! must—
  Designer infinite!—
Ah! must Thou char the wood ere Thou canst limn with it?
My freshness spent its wavering shower i' the dust;
And now my heart is as a broken fount,
Wherein tear-drippings stagnate, spilt down ever
  From the dank thoughts that shiver
Upon the sighful branches of my mind.
  Such is; what is to be?
The pulp so bitter, how shall taste the rind?
I dimly guess what Time in mists confounds;
Yet ever and anon a trumpet sounds
From the hid battlements of Eternity;
Those shaken mists a space unsettle, then
Round the half-glimpsed turrets slowly wash again.
  But not ere him who summoneth
  I first have seen, enwound
With glooming robes purpureal, cypress-crowned;
His name I know, and what his trumpet saith.
Whether man's heart or life it be which yields
  Thee harvest, must Thy harvest fields
  Be dunged with rotten death?

Now of that long pursuit
Comes on at hand the bruit;
That Voice is round me like a bursting sea:
"And is thy earth so marred,
Shattered in shard on shard?
Lo, all things fly thee, for thou fliest Me!
Strange, piteous, futile thing,
Wherefore should any set thee love apart?
Seeing none but I makes much of naught" (He said),
"And human love needs human meriting:
How hast thou merited—
Of all man's clotted clay the dingiest clot?
Alack, thou knowest not
How little worthy of any love thou art!
Whom wilt thou find to love ignoble thee
Save Me, save only Me?
All which I took from thee I did but take,
Not for thy harms,
But just that thou might'st seek it in My arms.
All which thy child's mistake
Fancies as lost, I have stored for thee at home:
Rise, clasp My hand, and come!"

Halts by me that footfall: [and here comes the punch line]
Is my gloom, after all,
Shade of His hand, outstretched caressingly?
"Ah, fondest, blindest, weakest,
I am He Whom thou seekest!
Thou dravest love from thee, who dravest Me."[57]

I want to compare that with a modern dream. As I said, the majority of flight dreams do not make it explicit that the dreamer is fleeing from the Self. But a few of them carry that implication rather strongly, as does the following dream, dreamt by a woman who was in conflict about whether to take seriously the full implication of the reality of the psyche.

She dreamt that she was in flight from a huge bird. She felt they were locked in a battle to the death, and she was out to destroy it. So she found herself engaged in a plot to destroy that bird even though she knew this effort was evil. Just as she expects to bring about the completion of the plot and destroy the bird, suddenly it dawns on her that she no longer has superiority over the bird. Now she is terrified. The tables have been turned, and

---

[57] Ibid., pp. 386ff.

she suddenly realizes that the huge screeching bird will get her. In order to keep the bird out, she has covered her entire house with a great plastic tent. But the bird has gotten in somehow and is silently waiting for her to rest when she expects it will kill her, peck out her eyes. She awakes terrified.

That is a good example of the attempt to flee from the Self.

Let us return to Jonah, who has gone to sea to get away from Yahweh. The story continues:

> But Yahweh unleashed a violent wind on the sea, and there was such a great storm at sea that the ship threatened to break up. The sailors took fright, and each of them called on his own god, and to lighten the ship they threw the cargo overboard. Jonah, however, had gone below and lain down in the hold and fallen fast asleep. The boatswain came upon him and said, "What do you men by sleeping? Get up! Call on your god! Perhaps he will spare us a thought, and not leave us to die." (1:4-6)

It's as though the elements themselves protest Jonah's flight from God, as though he is going against the cosmic current which is putting up a violent resistance to his going in the wrong direction.

Let me give you a personal example of that phenomenon. This took place before I decided to move from New York to California, when I was in the process of trying to make up my mind. I had occasion to make the trip back and forth from the east to the west coast several times. It was quite extraordinary. It was as though there were some obstacle going east. Each time I would go east something would go wrong. One time I got out to Los Angeles and there was an airline strike and I couldn't get back; I had great trouble in getting another reservation. I was delayed. On another trip we lost an engine and had to land in Detroit. Another time there was so much traffic in New York we couldn't land and had to go to Washington to refuel. Another time it was the last landing in the midst of a snowstorm. It was a very impressive experience, the difficulty in making it back east.

This sort of phenomenon is analogous, at least as I conceive it, to what happened to Jonah when he set out for Tarshish instead of setting out for Nineveh. There was this terrible storm.

Another feature is that Jonah is asleep during the storm. It is as though the tumult of the elements, the wild uproar of the outer world, has to develop because Jonah is asleep. It is as though—and we can often observe this psychologically—there is a reciprocal relation between the state of the ego and the state of the unconscious. It is not always true that when the ego is asleep the unconscious is in an uproar. There are plenty of examples where that is not the case at all. Often both the ego and the unconscious are asleep. But after a call from the Self, if the goes to sleep, then that puts the unconscious in a terrible uproar. And, vice versa, if the ego is in an uproar, then the unconscious is apt to provide something of a calming effect. So that if Jonah had carried more agitation consciously then the storm would not have to come up to awaken him.

The Book of Jonah continues, with the sailors speaking:

> Then they said to each other, "Come on, let us draw lots to find out who is responsible for bringing this evil on us." So they cast lots, and the lot fell to Jonah. Then they said to him, "Tell us, what is your business? Where do you come from? What is your country? What is your nationality?" He replied, "I am a Hebrew, and I worship Yahweh, the God of heaven, who made the sea and the land." The sailors were seized with terror at this and said, "What have you done?" They knew that he was trying to escape from Yahweh, because he had told them so. They then said, "What are we to do with you, to make the sea grow calm for us?" For the sea was growing rougher and rougher. He replied, "Take me and throw me into the sea, and then it will grow calm for you. For I can see it is my fault this violent storm has happened to you." (1:7-12)

This is the turning point of the story. After fleeing from his call, after taking ship to get as far away as possible, after escaping in sleep while the storm rages, Jonah now has a complete change of attitude, a *metanoia*. He repents. Now we hear a totally different statement from him. He takes responsibility, saying, "It's all my fault, do with me what is necessary to calm the storm"—which means that he accepts the need to go into the unconscious, to be dropped into the sea. And this acceptance immediately transforms Jonah from a fugitive to a hero.

The Willing Sacrifice

In the Gospels Christ was asked by the Pharisees to prove he was the Messiah by giving them a sign. And he said this wicked generation won't get any sign, except the sign of Jonah. (Matt. 12:39, 16:4; Luke 11:29) Now that is usually interpreted to refer to the resurrection, to the three days in the grave corresponding to the three days Jonah spent in the belly of the whale. However, I think there is a much closer and a much more satisfactory parallel in the attitude that Jonah takes in the midst of the storm: the attitude of willing sacrifice, of committing himself to the unconscious, realizing that it was his previous attitude that had stirred it up. We have here the emergence, then, of the sacrificial attitude of the ego in response to the activated unconscious.

The account continues:

> The sailors rowed hard in an effort to reach the shore, but in vain, since the sea grew still rougher for them. They then called on Yahweh and said, "O Yahweh, do not let us perish for taking this man's life; do not hold us guilty of innocent blood, for you, Yahweh, have acted as you have thought right." And taking hold of Jonah they threw him into the sea; and the sea grew calm again. At this the men were seized with dread of Yahweh; they offered a sacrifice to Yahweh and made vows.
>
> Yahweh had arranged that a great fish should be there to swallow Jonah; and Jonah remained in the belly of the fish for three days and three nights. (1:13-2:1)

I see this event as another very interesting example of the reciprocal relation between the ego and the unconscious. I urge you always to be on the lookout for this.

You see what has happened here. Jonah had a change of mind and told the sailors to throw him overboard. His willingness to descend into the unconscious then evoked a saving counterreaction from the unconscious— Yahweh sends a great fish to receive Jonah. Jung believes the unconscious seeks to compromise with the ego. The ego and the unconscious are often in a state of conflict. But if the ego makes some gesture of appeasement, of reconciliation, toward the unconscious, the unconscious responds in kind. It is quite willing to compromise as soon as the ego gives up its hostile attitude. Here we have an example of that phenomenon: Jonah, instead of drowning, is received quite hospitably by the great fish.

The Night Sea Journey

Jonah's changed attitude has turned the drama into another example of the myth of the hero devoured by a sea-monster. This is very relevant to the symbolism of Melville's *Moby-Dick*, which I've written about at length.[58] Behind this part of the Jonah story is the night sea journey motif. In *Sym-*

---

[58] [See *Melville's Moby-Dick: An American Nekyia*, chap. 5.—Ed.]

bols of Transformation, Jung quotes Frobenius's summary of many variations of this basic motif:

> A hero is devoured by a water-monster in the West. . . . The animal travels
> with him [inside] to the East. . . . Meanwhile, the hero lights a fire in the
> belly of the monster . . . and feeling hungry, cuts himself a piece of the
> heart. . . . Soon afterwards, he notices that the fish has glided on to dry land
> . . . ; he immediately begins to cut open the animal from within. . . . ; then he
> slips out. . . . It was so hot in the fish's belly that all his hair has fallen out.
> . . . The hero may at the same time free all those who were previously devoured by the monster.[59]

The Jonah story does not fit that precisely, but it is an approximation of it.

The symbolism depicts the archetypal theme of heroic incest, a purposeful descent into the maternal womb of the unconscious for the purpose of transformation and rebirth. The monster represents the primordial psyche in its natural, elemental and undifferentiated state. It is untamed animal energy, not yet available for the conscious civilized functioning of the ego. As long as that monster has not been entered and dealt with from within, the ego is in constant danger of being swallowed up by it. In other words, the ego is in danger of falling into possession by the primordial psyche, a danger symbolized by the image of incest.[60]

If the ego is particularly weak the threat can be one of actual psychosis. When I was working at Rockland State Hospital I recall seeing a patient who suffered periodic bouts of catatonic schizophrenia. He would have periods of remission and then revert to his psychosis. During a period of remission he dreamt that a huge whale was approaching him. He knew he was going to be swallowed and that there was nothing he could do to avoid it. He was helplessly awaiting his fate as he awoke. A few days after this dream he had a relapse of his schizophrenia, and during that time lost all contact with reality. This is what happens when a weak and regressive ego is swallowed by the monster.

There can be quite a different outcome when the ego approaches the monster in a purposeful way. Another patient with a very different prognosis had this dream:

---

[59] CW 5, par. 310.

[60] [For extensive commentary on the psychological significance of the incest motif, see Edinger, *The Mysterium Lectures,* pp. 38f., 84ff., 192f.—Ed.]

He sees a beautiful, seductive woman on a couch. She is naked and asks him to have intercourse with her. As he approaches she turns into a horrible, vulture-like monster whose genitals become a devouring mouth. The monster's mouth opens and begins to eat the dreamer's head. Instead of trying to fight his way out of her clutches, he hurries the process by literally crawling down her throat. Once inside he starts hitting her from within, and can hear her cries of pain. He then crawls right out of her in some awful birth process. From her entrails he rescues a tiny white figure—a wee gnomelike baby that begins growing as soon as it is released. It turns into a beautiful child, glowing and luminous, evoking an intense feeling of joy and exhilaration.

Clearly, this is a totally different event because it is a purposeful descent. Necessity has been turned into something purposeful by being consciously chosen. The result is that the emergent Self grows out of the experience.

The content of this particular dream, of fighting or clawing the creature from within, is reminiscent of a Gnostic monster myth about the descent of Hibil. It is described by Hans Jonas:

Karkûm the great flesh-mountain said unto me [this is the hero speaking]: Go, or I shall devour thee. When he spoke thus to me, I was in a casing of swords, sabres, lances, knives, and blades, and I said unto him: Devour me. Then . . . he swallowed me half-way: then he spewed me forth. . . . He spewed venom out of his mouth, for his bowels, his liver, and his reins [kidneys] were cut to pieces.[61]

What we have here, the casing of knives and blades, symbolizes the sharp, discriminating power of consciousness, which can break up and dismember the unconscious monster, making its energy available to the ego.

This myth is an example of the fact that light is a poison to darkness. So if a conscious entity knowingly offers itself up to be devoured by the darkness it is administering a poison pill to the dark, because it attacks it from within. Another way of saying this is that by consciousness descending into the unconsciousness it sets a transformation process in operation. This can only happen, however, when it is done deliberately. The ego that regressively falls into the unconscious has the opposite effect; then the light is poisoned by the darkness. That is totally different.

An example of this theme comes from Cyril of Jerusalem, one of the Church Fathers, who said that Christ's body was a bait for the devil. On swallowing the bait the devil found it so indigestible that he had to yield it

---

[61] *The Gnostic Religion,* p. 121.

up again, in the same way as the whale spewed forth Jonah. Another version of this same image is the crucifix being used as a bait to catch Leviathan (opposite). It is the same idea, that purposeful consciousness, if it is swallowed by the dark monster, will poison that monster from within.

The Book of Jonah continues:

> From the belly of the fish he prayed to Yahweh, his God; he said:
>
> "Out of my distress I cried to Yahweh
> and he answered me;
> from the belly of Sheol I cried.
> and you have heard my voice.
> You cast me into the abyss, into the heart of the sea,
> and the flood surrounded me.
> All your waves, your billows,
> washed over me.
> And I said: I am cast out from your sight.
> How shall I ever look again
> on your holy Temple?"
> The waters surrounded me right to my throat,
> the abyss was all around me.
> The seaweed was wrapped around my head
> at the roots of the mountains.
> I went down into the countries underneath the earth,
> to the peoples of the past.
> But you lifted my life from the pit,
> Yahweh, my God.
> While my soul was fainting within me,
> I remembered Yahweh,
> and my prayer came before you
> into your holy Temple.
> Those who serve worthless idols
> forfeit the grace that was theirs.
>
> "But I, with a song of praise,
> will sacrifice to you.
> The vow I have made, I will fulfill.
> Salvation comes from Yahweh." (2:2-10)

As you will have noticed, the Jerusalem Bible.has set out for us where all this comes from. It is a mosaic of quotations from the Psalms. The marginal references locate them all for us. I think that indicates that in the belly of the whale it is as though Jonah has lost his own individual voice, and is now speaking in the archetypal voice, the transpersonal voice.

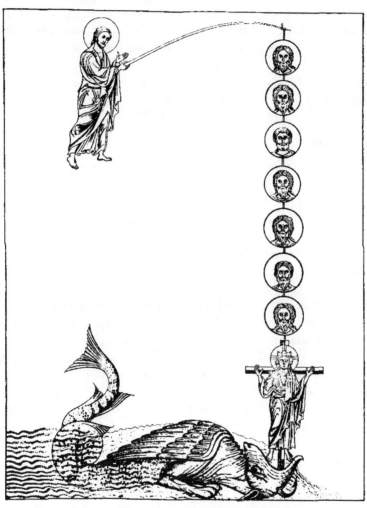

Capture of the Leviathan, with the crucifix as bait.
(From Herrad of Landsberg, *Hortus deliciarum,* 12th century;
New York Public Library; in CW 12, fig. 28.)

It reminds me of the fact that when Christ was being tempted by the devil—there were three temptations—his response in each case was a quotation. He did not give a personal response. He said, "It is written." And I think most of those responses were from the Psalms too.[62] It is as though, when one is really in a state of extreme psychological urgency, in the belly of the whale, so to speak, when the devil really is behind the temptation, the only safe attitude to have is one that is founded on archetypal reality as opposed to ego reality. That is how I understand Jonah's prayer: what he says in the belly of the whale is not the ego talking, it is scripture.

In the Belly of the Whale

It is interesting to see what the legendary material has done with the story of Jonah. Certainly we know that, psychologically, being swallowed by a whale can have either progressive or regressive implications, as I've indicated—depending on whether the ego attitude is an active or a passive one. If it is active then it is a heroic descent into the unconscious. If it is a passive attitude, then it is a dangerous regressive phenomenon of being swallowed up. That regressive aspect is alluded to in a legend reported by Louis Ginzberg.[63] According to this legend, Jonah was very comfortable in the belly of the whale. He found it very agreeable. The text reads: "He was as comfortable inside the whale as in a spacious synagogue." I cannot help but think that that is a reference to the comfortable, collective containment of *participation mystique* in a traditional religious setting. And since Jonah had no incentive to leave, God was obliged to transform the whale into a second, smaller fish, where he was quite cramped. In that second fish he repented and prayed for deliverance.

Another legend has it that the fish took Jonah on a guided tour:

> The fish carried Jonah withersoever there was a sight to be seen. He showed him the river from which the ocean flows, showed him the spot at which the Israelites crossed the Red Sea, showed him Gehenna and Sheol, and many other mysteries and wonderful places.[64]

---

[62] [The synoptic account of the temptation is in Matt. 4:1-11, Mark 1:12-13 and Luke 4:1-13. Christ's words are from Deut. as well as from Psalm 91:11-12.—Ed.]
[63] *Legends of the Bible,* pp. 605f.
[64] Ibid.

In other words, Jonah's descent into the whale was an initiation into the mysteries. Paracelsus says much the same thing, that Jonah saw "mighty mysteries" in the belly of the whale.[65]

Looking at it that way, then, we could say that Jonah's initiation into the mysteries completes his change of attitude. Yahweh now answers his prayer and repeats Jonah's assignment:

Yahweh spoke to the fish, which then vomited Jonah onto the shore.

The word of Yahweh was addressed a second time to Jonah: "Up!" he said, "Go to Nineveh, the great city, and preach to them as I told you to." Jonah set out and went to Nineveh in obedience to the word of Yahweh. Now Nineveh was a city great beyond compare, it took three days to cross it. Jonah went on into the city, making a day's journey. He preached in these words, "Only forty days more and Nineveh is going to be destroyed." And the people of Nineveh believed in God; they proclaimed a fast and put on sackcloth, from the greatest to the least. The news reached the king of Nineveh, who rose from his throne, took off his robe, put on sackcloth and sat down in ashes. A proclamation was then promulgated throughout Nineveh, by decree of the king and his ministers, as follows: "Men and beasts, herds and flocks, are to taste nothing; they must not eat, they must not drink water. All are to put on sackcloth and call on God with all their might; and let everyone renounce his evil behavior and the wicked things he has done. Who knows if God will not change his mind and relent, if he will not renounce his burning wrath, so that we do not perish?" God saw their efforts to renounce their evil behaviour. And God relented: he did not inflict on them the disaster which he had threatened. (2:11-3:10)

Nineveh repents. What would this mean in individual psychology? I think it means that Nineveh represents a layer of the collective psyche between Jonah, the ego, and Yahweh, the Self. We might think of Nineveh as an aspect of Leviathan, the whale that swallowed Jonah. Just as Jonah's descent into the monster has transformed him, so—by implication—it has also transformed the whale, the darkness—because I have told you how when light descends into darkness it changes it. Likewise, Jonah's penetration into, and preaching in, Nineveh has transformed the collective and brought about repentance.

I think we can say that there is a symbolic equation between Nineveh and the whale Leviathan. I can use the authority of Thomas Hobbes for

---

[65] Quoted in *Symbols of Transformation,* CW 5, par. 509.

this. He likens the political state to Leviathan. I would not use that example if were not also symbolically accurate. But it is. Hobbes says in his introduction to his famous treatise on political philosophy:

> For by Art is created that great Leviathan called a Common-wealth or State,
> . . . which is but an Artificial Man, though of greater stature and strength
> than the Natural Man.[66]

That is how I understand the city of Nineveh. It is another version of what is symbolized by the whale.

It is interesting to note the Jonah-ego's reaction to Nineveh's transformation and rescue from God's wrath. The passage continues:

> Jonah was very indignant at this; he fell into a rage. He prayed to Yahweh
> and said, "Ah! Yahweh, is not this just as I said would happen when I was
> still at home? That is why I went and fled to Tarshish: I knew that you were
> a God of tenderness and compassion, slow to anger, rich in graciousness,
> relenting from evil. So now Yahweh, please take away my life, for I might
> as well be dead as go on living." (4:1-4)

Keep in mind the rule of reciprocity that I spoke of earlier.[67] I think Nineveh's wickedness and ungodliness has been transferred to the ego, Jonah. That is one way of putting it. The other way of putting it is that Yahweh's wrath has been transferred to Jonah, the ego, because both Nineveh and Yahweh are undergoing a *metanoia*. They are both repenting of their previous attitude. This repentance on the part of Nineveh and Yahweh is accompanied by Jonah's becoming conscious of these power motivations which had previously been unconscious. Yahweh was in a state of wrath at Nineveh's wickedness. Nineveh repents and Yahweh loses his wrath, but that process of change involves the transfer of the wrath and the wickedness to the ego. That is how the psychological transformation process takes place. It just does not happen magically. It has to be transmitted through the conscious organ which is the ego. So Jonah is burdened with the vengeful desire that has now left Yahweh.

You might say that since Jonah is carrying the attitude of vengeance and the state of depression that its frustration generates, this allows Yahweh to manifest Himself in His loving and merciful aspect. That is how it

---

[66] *Leviathan*, p. 8.
[67] Above, pp. 125f.

would be seen if we keep in mind the notion of the reciprocal relation between the ego and the Self.

The text continues:

> Yahweh replied, "Are you right to be angry?" Jonah then went out of the city and sat down to the east of the city. There he made himself a shelter and sat under it in the shade, to see what would happen to the city. Then Yahweh God arranged that a Castor-oil plant should grow up over Jonah to give shade for his head and soothe his ill-humor; Jonah was delighted with the castor-oil plant. But at dawn the next day, God arranged that a worm should attack the castor-oil plant—and it withered. Next when the sun rose, God arranged that there should be a scorching east wind; the sun beat down so hard on Jonah's head that he was overcome and he begged for death, saying, "I might as well be dead as go on living." God said to Jonah, "Are you right to be angry about the castor-oil plant?" He replied, "I have every right to be angry, to the point of death." Yahweh replied, "You are only upset about a castor-oil plant which cost you no labor, which you did not make grow, which sprouted in a night and has perished in a night. And am I not to feel sorry for Nineveh, the great city, in which there are more than a hundred and twenty thousand people who cannot tell their right hand from their left, to say nothing of all the animals?" (4:5-11)

Yahweh's wrath, corresponding symbolically to Leviathan, has been transformed by the ego's descent into the unconscious. This descent into the unconscious does darken the ego, because it takes on aspects of the primordial psyche. That is what the descent means. However, the inner mixture of ego consciousness with the divine darkness has the effect of transforming the darkness, the unconscious, which is to say, as previously suggested, that God needs the assistance of the human ego to become conscious of Himself.

9
Nahum; Habakkuk; Zephaniah; Haggai; Zechariah; Malachi

I want to say just a few words about each of these very brief books.

Nahum

Nahum is a prophet about whom nothing at all is known. The chief content of his prophecy is the fall of Nineveh, which was conquered by Babylonia in 612 B.C., so presumably he prophesied sometime before that date.

Probably what is most impressive in the Book of Nahum is the striking description of Yahweh in the first chapter where he is described practically as the personification of vengeance. Listen to this:

> Yahweh is a jealous and vengeful God,
> Yahweh avenges, he is full of wrath;
> Yahweh takes vengeance on his foes,
> he stores up fury for his enemies.
> Yahweh is slow to anger but immense in power.
> Most surely Yahweh will not leave the guilty unpunished.
> In storm and whirlwind he takes his way
> . . . .
> . . . Bashan and Carmel wither,
> the green of Lebanon fades.
> The mountains tremble before him,
> the hills reel;
> the earth collapses before him,
> the world and all who live in it.
> His fury—who can withstand it?
> Who can endure his burning wrath?
> His anger pours out like fire
> and the rocks break to pieces before him. (1:2-6)

Then it changes and says:

> Yahweh is good; he is a stronghold
> in the day of distress;
> he calls to mind those who trust in him
> when the flood overtakes them.
> Those who defy him he will destroy utterly,
> he will pursue his foes into the darkness. (1:7-8)

I think this is another example of what we have noted a number of times before, namely that affect comes from Yahweh. In this case it is the affect of the power motive, because that is what vengeance is associated with. Vengeance specifically returns hurt for hurt. It is the organism's primordial response to an agent that has inflicted pain on it. It strikes back like a rattlesnake that has been disturbed. That is the nature of the primordial psyche.

Psychologically, the crucial question is whether or not the ego is identified with that affect. Because when it is, it just perpetuates the cycle: the primitive in me responds to having pain inflicted on me, I inflict pain in turn, the primitive Yahweh in the person I inflict pain on responds in turn, and it goes on endlessly because there is no consciousness to break it up. You see the primordial psyche operating on a collective level in phenomena of all kinds. In politics, especially international politics, nations don't seem to function at the level of individual psychology, rather they function at the level of the primitive collective psyche. The object lesson is laid out for all to see in the never-ending quarrels and disputes between countries.

Habakkuk

Nothing is known about Habakkuk either. This book too was probably written around 600 B.C. The chief theme in Habakkuk is the prophet's dialogue with Yahweh in which he asks the age old question, "How long, Yahweh? How long must we put up with evil unpunished?" And Yahweh replies that trouble is coming to evil doers. That's about it.

Zephaniah

Next comes the Book of Zephaniah. This prophecy occurred during the reign of King Josiah, which puts it between 639 and 608 B.C.—in the same general range as the other two, a few decades earlier. In this book the major image is the Great Day of Yahweh, which you will recall from the earlier lecture on the Book of Isaiah.[68] I will read you a little description of that in Zephaniah:

> The great day of Yahweh is near,
> near, and coming with all speed.
> How bitter the sound of the day of Yahweh,
> the day when the warrior shouts his cry of war.

---

[68] Above, pp. 16ff.

A day of wrath, that day,
a day of distress and agony,
A day of ruin and of devastation,
a day of darkness and gloom,
a day of cloud and blackness,
a day of trumpet blast and battle cry
against fortified town
and high corner tower.
I am going to bring such distress on men
that they will grope like the blind
(because they have sinned against Yahweh);
their blood will be scattered like dust,
their corpses like dung.

. . . .

On the day of the anger of Yahweh,
in the fire of his jealousy,
all the earth will be consumed.
For he means to destroy, yes, to make an end
of all the inhabitants of the earth. (1:14-18)

This image has come up several times, that of the great day of destruction. It then finally goes through an enantiodromia and turns into the Messianic age, which I'll speak more about later.

Haggai

The Book of Haggai was written in 520 B.C., at the end of the Babylonian captivity, when the exiles had already been allowed to return to Jerusalem. In Haggai the chief theme is that Yahweh orders his temple to be rebuilt.

Zechariah

Zechariah was a contemporary of Haggai. They worked together to promote the rebuilding of the temple. He had some quite interesting visions that are psychologically significant. In the first vision, in the first chapter, he sees Yahweh's four horses that patrol the world. They are associated with the four directions, the four points of the compass. It is one of the numerous examples of the deity represented as a quaternity.

In the second chapter, there is a vision of the four horns that scattered Israel, another manifestation of Yahweh as a quaternity. Zechariah is shown a man who is measuring Jerusalem, and Yahweh says the walls are not going to be reconstructed in this Jerusalem, because he, Yahweh, is going to be the walls: "I will be a wall of fire for her." (2:9) This is taken by the commentators and later reflectors on the text as a reference to the Messianic Jerusalem, rather than the concrete Jerusalem.

In the third chapter a priest is standing at the court of heaven between the angel of Yahweh and Satan, which is to say between the opposites. The priest is given clean clothes to replace his dirty ones. This is the sort of theme that comes up sometimes in dreams occurring around the occasion of a death, where one of the survivors of the deceased is apt to dream that the dead person has changed clothes, put on clean new clothes, something of that sort.

Also in chapter 3 there is the particularly important image of the stone with the seven eyes. This particular image was used by the alchemists; whenever they found a reference to the stone that had sacred implications, they could apply that to their Philosophers' Stone. This stone with the seven eyes in it is an important image of the Self. It is a symbol of Yahweh as stone and also as the eye of God; in other words, the capacity of the unconscious to see the ego. In this case it is a sevenfold seeing.

The same image is elaborated in a little different way in chapter 4, where Zechariah sees a lamp stand with seven lamps on it, and is told that the seven lamps are the seven eyes of Yahweh. These are relevant amplification images whenever one encounters dreams in which the dreamer is being looked at from some strange or unusual place.

In chapter 5 there is the image of the flying scroll which is God's curse that is being distributed across the earth. And also the image of a woman in a bushel who was a personification of wickedness and who is flying off to Shinar. It is as though evil is somehow undergoing a consolidation. It is being gathered up from the land and is crystallizing out into a specific personification: a woman who is being carried off to Shinar in a grain basket. There she will become queen of the enemy territory, so to speak. On the one hand it represents a dissociation of the evil from the good. On the other hand it is a *separatio* process in which the opposites are being explicitly distinguished from each other.

In chapter 6 we have the vision of the four chariots that come out from between two mountains. One chariot is drawn by red horses, one by black horses, one by white horses and one by piebald, spotted horses. They are going out in the direction of the four winds. Here is the theme of the three and the four again. There are four, three of them are clear cut, and one of them is mixed up and contaminated. It is not clean, not pure.

Malachi

In the Book of Malachi, as in some of the others, Yahweh announces his coming. In the third chapter Yahweh says,

> Behold, I will send my messenger, and he shall prepare the way before me: and the Lord, whom ye seek, shall suddenly come to his temple, even the messenger of the covenant, whom ye delight in: behold, he shall come, saith the Lord of hosts.
>
> But who may abide the day of his coming? and who shall stand when he appeareth? for he is like a refiners fire. (3:1-2, AV)

Here is how this last book of the Old Testament begins, with Yahweh making this pronouncement to Malachi:

> I have shown my love for you, says Yahweh. But you ask, "How have you shown your love?" [And the reply is:] Was not Esau Jacob's brother?—it is Yahweh who speaks; yet I showed my love for Jacob and my hatred for Esau. I turned his towns into a wilderness and his heritage into desert pastures. Should Edom say, "We have been struck down but we will rebuild our ruins," this is the reply of Yahweh Sabaoth: Let them build! I will pull down. They shall be known as Unholy Land and Nation-with-which-Yahweh-is-angry-for-ever. Your eyes are going to see this and you will say, "Yahweh is mighty beyond the borders of Israel." (1:2-5)

This is a striking statement to come at this point in the Old Testament. It leads into a paper that I have mentioned before, "Amalek, the Eternal Adversary," by Myron Gubitz.[69] I want to review at this point some of the contents of that paper. I consider it quite an important contribution. It speaks directly to the character of Yahweh, and how he can say things such as I just read.

The Eternal Enmity

The theme that runs throughout the Old Testament, starting from Jacob and Esau, is the eternal enmity, first between "Israel" (that's Jacob's later name) and Esau, followed by the eternal enmity between Israel and the Amalekites. In the seventeenth chapter of Exodus we first hear of the Amalekites. They attacked Israel at Rephidim and Israel prevailed as long as Moses' arms were lifted up, you remember, and when his arms became

---

[69] [See Edinger, *The Bible and the Psyche,* p. 36.—Ed.]

tired, he had to have somebody to support them, because as soon as they fell down then the Amalekites prevailed. After that engagement Yahweh made this pronouncement: "I shall wipe out the memory of Amalek from under heaven." (Exod. 17:15) He told Moses, "Lay hold of the banner of Yahweh! Yahweh is at war with Amalek from age to age." (Exod. 17: 16) Later, in Deuteronomy, Moses says:

> Remember how Amalek treated you . . . . When Yahweh your God had granted you peace from all the enemies surrounding you in the land Yahweh your god is giving to possess as an inheritance, you are to blot out the memory of Amalek from under heaven. Do not forget. (Deut. 25:17-19)

That is what Moses reminded Israel of on that occasion.

Then in the fifteenth chapter of I Samuel, you will remember that Yahweh told Saul to attack and destroy the Amalekites, and put them all to death. Everything was to go under the ban. But Saul spared King Agag, and as a result of that disobedience Yahweh withdrew his favor from Saul. Agag was the ancestor of Haman, the villain of the book of Esther. Haman is the conventional and legendary personification of all the evil forces plotting to destroy the Jews.

In his paper, Gubitz reports that as a child he heard a Rabbi's sermon in which the Rabbi said that because Agag was permitted by Saul to live, therefore his descendant Haman came into existence, causing the terrible troubles at the time of Esther, and the modern descendant of Haman is Hitler. That made a big impression on Gubitz. His very fine paper likely came out of that childhood reaction, much as Jung's splendid essay on the Trinity might be traced back to his dissatisfied reaction to his father. When Jung was waiting for the lesson on the Trinity—because it was very interesting to him—and they came to that lesson his father said, "'We now come to the Trinity, but we'll skip that, for I really understand nothing of it myself."[70] Jung had to fill in that gap, so to speak.

Now who was Amalek? Amalek was the grandson of Esau—a direct descendent of Esau. So Amalek carried on the revenge of Esau for Jacob's crime against him, of stealing his birthright. Esau was cheated and robbed and laden with shadow projection. His grandson Amalek personifies the vengeful resentment at such mistreatment. It sounds strangely like the Yahweh I quoted a few minutes ago, does it not? So Amalek represents

---

[70] *Memories, Dreams, Reflections,* p. 53.

the dissociated vengeance complex, resulting from the primal crime that lies in the depths of the Judeo-Christian psyche which attacks the ego and in turn is viciously repressed. They are at perpetual war, forever, age after age. The material spells that out explicitly.

Gubitz makes this startling analogy. He says that the Amalekites' first attack on Israel, which is an expression of revenge for the crime against Esau, was Esau's proposed final solution to the Jacob problem. This was then followed by Yahweh's projected final solution of the Amalekite problem. Gubbitz expresses the psychological implications very well. I want to quote a passage. He says that Jacob's superceding of Esau was an advance in development:

> But, as is almost inevitably the case with the process of change, that step disrupted an existing unity, and thus created a new dichotomy.
>
> In other words, Jacob's "progress" had its price—and from this perspective the biblical tale is a mythic statement of the basic human truth that each move into a new developmental phase usually is paid for in guilt, anxiety, suffering, often blood. On the personal level, we all experience this through the guilt feelings and anxiety which almost inevitably accompany a child's progressive escape from parental influence and domination. To make this kind of anxiety subjectively bearable we are often forced to project it, to see it as an external threat rather than as the inherent tragedy of man's estate, a result of our own unavoidable fragmentation in the course of development. Perhaps this is something like what took place in the Israelite psyche: the burden of guilt and anxiety which accompanied the commitment to a new spiritual and psychological orientation was projected outward, first onto Esau, and then onto his disruptive offspring Amalek.[71]

The very interesting feature here is that the split and the shadow projection that is put onto Amalek is initiated by Yahweh—which means it comes from the Self, not the ego. It is stated explicitly that Yahweh is the one in perpetual enmity with Amalek. On several occasions Israel pays dearly by treating Amalek a little too kindly—to the very end of the Old Testament, because we've reached the end and I'm now giving an amplification of a quote from the last book, Malachi. So to the very end Yahweh remains the God of Jacob and the hater of Esau. He wants to exterminate all Esau's descendants. In other words, Yahweh does not know anything about shadow projection. The dynamism of the Self generates a split into a

---

[71] "Amalek, the Eternal Adversary," pp. 42f.

loved one, Jacob or Israel, and a hated one, Esau. This same archetypal fact duplicates itself in Christian symbolism where God generates two sons, the good one, Christ, and the bad one, Satan. It is exactly the same archetype, which means that what we are dealing with here is absolutely basic to the development of the psyche, not something that could just as well be different, some little mistake. This is primary.

Of course, as soon as the ego begins to get a glimmer of these basic facts—and I guess the child does not have to be very old, two or three, before it gets such a glimmer—it will want to identify with Jacob, the chosen one, and have nothing to do with Esau, the hated one. There is no question about that. It will not always succeed in that desire, but that is what it will want to do. But if that identification with Jacob becomes a prolonged and systematized psychological stance, then of course Esau has to be projected, because it still exists; it is still a psychic entity and it will be lurking around in that projection waiting to get revenge.

You see, the Jacob-identified ego is in perpetual danger of falling victim to the projected, revengeful Esau. This is the terrible psychological danger of the Jews and of the Christians after them. Because the Christians tried to steal Israel's inheritance and claimed to be the spiritual Israel. That is their claim, and by making that claim they take on the same problem, it is exactly the same thing. They identify with Jacob, and then they set up to be the victims of whoever is carrying the Esau projection.

Jacob and Esau are archetypal images or motifs. We are now, for the first time in human history, in a position to be conscious of this level of psychic reality. It has never been available before. We can now perceive that the ego should identify with neither of these archetypes, neither Jacob nor Esau. They represent the objects of the love and the wrath of God, and the ego's proper position is to stand between them. The way Jung puts it in "Answer to Job" is like this:

> God has a terrible double aspect: a sea of grace [the way he feels toward Jacob] is met by a seething lake of fire [the way he feels toward Esau], and the light of love glows with a fierce dark heat of which it is said . . . — it burns but gives no light.[72]

So Jacob is the recipient of God's love and grace, and Esau is the recipient of his fiery wrath.

---

[72] *Psychology and Religion,* CW 11, par. 733.

If you are really going to perceive these facts in depth then you may no longer make such identifications. You can no longer be a "good Jew" as opposed to the ignorant, Godless *goyim.* You can no longer be a "good Christian" over against the unbelievers. You can no longer be a Marxist over and against the Capitalist. And also, of course, you can no longer be a good conscious Jungian against all the unconscious other psychologists. These are all expressions of identification with Jacob over against Esau. When you identify with Jacob, you inevitably constellate Esau somewhere inside or outside, or both, and are in a state of constant war as a result.

This is the state that the Judeo-Christian psyche has been in from the beginning. And the time has now come when we have to get out of it. We have to get out of the identification with Jacob. And in order to get out of it, we have to go through its opposite. In order to get out of identification with one side of the pair of opposites, we have to go through—at least briefly—an identification or connection with the contrary. In this case it would mean a connection or identification with Esau. If Jacob is the Godly one, the one in positive relation to God, then Esau is the atheist, the one at war against God. Something of this sort is what the collective psyche is in the process of going through.

Nietzsche, as usual, has put it brilliantly. I want to read you another passage from *The Gay Science:*

> As a philosopher, Schopenhauer was the *first* admitted and inexorable atheist among us Germans. . . . The ungodliness of existence was for him something given, palpable, indisputable; he always lost his philosopher's composure and became indignant when he saw anyone hesitate or mince matters at this point. This is the locus of his whole integrity; unconditional and honest atheism is simply the *presupposition* of the way he poses his problem—being a triumph achieved finally and with great difficulty by the European conscience, being the most faithful act of two thousand years of discipline for truth that in the end forbids itself the *lie* in faith in God.
>
> You see what it was that really triumphed over the Christian God: Christian morality itself, the concept of truthfulness that was understood ever more rigorously, the father confessor's refinement of the Christian conscience, translated and sublimated into a scientific conscience, into intellectual cleanliness at any price. Looking at nature as if it were proof of the goodness and governance of God; interpreting history in honor of some divine reason, as a continual testimony of a moral world order and ultimate moral purposes; interpreting one's own experiences as pious people have

long enough interpreted theirs, as if everything were providential, a hint designed and ordained for the sake of the salvation of the soul—that is *all over* now, that has man's conscience *against* it, that is considered indecent and dishonest by every more refined conscience. . . . In this severity, if anywhere, we are *good* Europeans and heirs of Europe's longest and most courageous self-overcoming.

As we thus reject the Christian interpretation and condemn its "meaning" like counterfeit, *Schopenhauer's* question immediately comes to us in a terrifying way: *Has existence any meaning at all?* It will require a few centuries before this question can even be heard completely and in its full depth.[73]

That is a wonderful vision. But in fact the relocation of meaning has not taken so long after all. The wonderful gift of Jungian psychology is the teaching that when concrete religious faith is lost, meaning is still to be discovered by becoming conscious.

Indeed, the only way to make the transition from the meaning one experiences in the containment of a concrete faith and identification with Jacob—the transition from that to the individual experience of the reality of the transpersonal psyche—*is* through the loss of faith. You have to go through the experience of meaninglessness, which is arrived at by being completely honest in the terms Nietzsche described.

And even with an experience of the Self, there is no return to comfortable security or guarantee of meaningfulness. Jung certainly gives us no comfortable reassurance on this point. Here is what he has to say:

The world into which we are born is brutal and cruel, and at the same time of divine beauty. Which element we think outweighs the other, whether meaninglessness or meaning, is a matter of temperament. If meaninglessness were absolutely preponderant, the meaningfulness of life would vanish to an increasing degree with each step in our development. But that is—or seems to me—not the case. Probably, as in all metaphysical questions, both are true: Life is—or has—meaning and meaninglessness. I cherish the anxious hope that meaning will preponderate and win the battle.[74]

That does not sound like comfortable certainty to me. The way I read it is that an explicit ultimate meaning is not built into the unconscious, but rather is created by the joint efforts and the encounters that take place between the ego and the Self. It is not quite true to say that the ego finds

---

[73] In Walter Kaufmann, trans. and ed., *The Gay Science,* pp. 307f.
[74] *Memories, Dreams, Reflections,* p. 358.

meaning. It is probably more accurate to say it creates meaning out of its urge to survive. For instance, in the second chapter of Malachi Yahweh says to the priests: "If you do not find it in your heart to glorify my name, I will send the curse on you." (2:2)

The experience indicated by that statement is an incentive to seek meaning, to look for it, to strive to create it. It is saying that Yahweh needs his name to be glorified, that he cannot do it for himself. He needs an ego; he needs a mediator. To the extent that the mutual effort succeeds, meaning is created. In fact that is one way one might formulate the purpose of individual human existence: to create meaning. Each person is a crucible in which potentially a unique life meaning is created. Meaning and consciousness are analogous in that image.

This understanding gives superlative importance to the conscious ego. The only trustworthy thing in the universe is a really conscious individual human being. We are all relatively untrustworthy because we have an unconscious. But the more conscious individual, the more reliable and trustworthy a person is, and how Yahweh energy is going to manifest itself, whether it manifests creatively or destructively, depends very largely on the nature and degree of consciousness of the ego through which it expresses itself.

Yahweh As a Dark Cloud

I want to say a few things about Yahweh and his presence as it manifests in the cloud. In II Chronicles we read that when Solomon's temple had been completed, Yahweh took possession of it, and that a cloud filled the temple. That's the basic image. Now, in the third chapter of Malachi, Yahweh speaks these words:

> Look, I am going to send my messenger to prepare a way before me. And the Lord you are seeking will suddenly enter his Temple; and the angel of the covenant whom you are longing for, yes he is coming, says Yahweh Sabaoth. Who will be able to resist the day of his coming? Who will remain standing when he appears? For he is like the refiner's fire and the fullers' alkali. He will take his seat as refiner and purifier; he will purify the sons of Levi and refine them like gold and silver, and then they will make the offering to Yahweh as it should be made. (3:1-4)

So here again is another reference to Yahweh's entering the temple. And here the coming to his temple is equivalent to what's called the Day of Yahweh, which you will recall means Judgment Day.

Psychologically we can understand this imagery to refer to the day when the ego finally meets the activated Self. The symbolism of this event is often negative. The negative is implied in this passage too where it says "Who will remain standing? Who will be able to resist?" The Authorized Version, and Handel's in the *Messiah,* reads: "Who may abide the day of his coming?" It often has a strongly negative cast because the ego at that moment is confronted with all its illusions, presumptions and unconscious errors. And therefore what we often have symbolically in the image of the coming of the cloud is what comes as a black cloud.

James Kirsch, in the book I have mentioned, *The Reluctant Prophet,* goes into some very interesting dreams of a nineteenth-century Rabbi who predicted twentieth-century events. And one of those dreams is of a black thunder cloud coming over Europe from the east. That is an example of Yahweh coming to his temple.

Another example is in a science fiction book, *The Black Cloud,* written by the astronomer Fred Hoyle. Jung refers to it in an appendix to his essay on flying saucers.[75] The basic story is that a black cloud comes from the outer reaches of the universe and finally settles in between the earth and the sun. It came in to recharge its battery, so to speak, from the sun. And it almost freezes the earth to death. A couple of scientists try to communicate with this cloud. It turns out it to be intelligent, but they go mad because they can't stand the advanced contents that this intelligence pours into them. I want to read you a little bit from what Jung says about this book. Remember we are talking about the image of Yahweh coming to his temple; in this case the black cloud comes into the vicinity of earth.

> Just as earthly life is largely wiped out by the collision with the cloud, so the psyche and the life of the two scientists are destroyed by the collision with the unconscious. For although the *rotundum* is a totality symbol, it usually encounters a consciousness that is not prepared for it and does not understand it, indeed is bound to misunderstand it and therefore cannot tolerate it, because it perceives the totality only in projected form, outside itself, and cannot integrate it as a subjective phenomenon.[76]

What happens next is that nuclear bombs are shot at the cloud, and this disrupts its nervous system and discourages it from hanging around. It just

---

[75] "Flying Saucers: A Modern Myth," *Civilization in Transition,* CW 10, pars. 810ff.

[76] Ibid., par. 814.

drifts off into space again. Jung notes:

> This means, psychologically: the unconscious, after gaining a certain amount of energy, sinks back again to its former distance. The final outcome is depressing: human consciousness and life in general suffer an incalculable loss through an incomprehensible *lusus naturae* [freak of nature] that lacks all human meaning, a "frolic" on a cosmic scale.[77]

Jung concludes: "It remains to be seen whether this melancholy outcome is a prophecy or a subjective confession."[78]

Another example of a black cloud comes from Marie-Louise von Franz's edition of *Aurora Consurgens*. This is from the sixth chapter:

> Beholding from afar off I saw a great cloud looming black over the whole earth, which had absorbed the earth and covered my soul, (because) the waters had come in even under her, wherefore they were putrefied and corrupted before the face of the lower hell and the shadow of death, for a tempest hath overwhelmed me; . . . there is no health in my flesh and all my bones are troubled before the face of my iniquity. For this cause have I laboured with crying, my jaws are become hoarse; who is the man that liveth, knowing and understanding, delivering my soul from the hand of hell?[79]

Here is the *Sapientia Dei;* it is an image of the *anima mundi* overcome by the *nigredo,* which is at the same time the dark manifestation of Yahweh coming to his temple. And it brings with it the full impact of the unassimilated shadow.

I think it is important to be familiar with this symbolism because it helps one to endure the dark aspects of the Self when one encounters them, especially when images from the unconscious make it clear that the totality is involved. The Self is bringing the darkness, or one could say that the dark aspect of the Self is expressing itself. No level of psychological development protects one from such experiences.

Jung himself is an example of that. In a letter written in the last year of his life, Jung speaks of his depression.

> Your letter [he is answering Eugene Wolf] has reached me at a time which was the tail end of a series of disappointments which has brought me down to the lowest ebb of feeling I ever experienced. The evil was that I had to

---

[77] Ibid., par. 818.
[78] Ibid., par. 819.
[79] *Aurora Consurgens,* p. 57.

realize the inability to fight my battles any more. I have to pay the tribute to my old age and accept the beatings lying down. I have to understand that I was unable to make the people see what I am after. I am practically alone. There are a few who understand this and that. But almost nobody that sees the whole. Why should I live any longer? My wife is dead. My children are all away and married. I have failed in my foremost task: to open people's eyes to the fact that man has a soul and that there is a buried treasure in the field and that our religion and philosophy is in a lamentable state. Why indeed should I continue to exist?[80]

That was Jung's experience of the dark cloud of Yahweh in the very last year of his life. His spirits picked up again, but I think it is important for us lesser mortals to know that Jung had such experiences to the end.

The Messianic Age

Throughout our reading of the Old Testament we have come across passages that are considered Messianic texts, pertaining to a future, universal king or an anointed one who will inaugurate a new age. I want to conclude my remarks, for tonight and for the whole course, by speaking of this idea of the Messianic age, which the Old Testament alludes to and which legendary material has picked up and elaborated.

In Isaiah there was the passage describing the Messianic age in which the wolf would live with the lamb, and the panther would lie down with the kid, and the calf and lion cubs would feed together, and a little boy would lead them (11:6ff.). In Hosea it is described this way:

> When that day comes I will make a treaty on her behalf with
>   the wild animals,
> with the birds of heaven and the creeping things of the earth;
> I will break bow, sword and battle in the country,
> and make her sleep secure.
> I will betroth you to myself for ever,
> betroth you with integrity and justice,
> with tenderness and love;
> I will betroth you to myself with faithfulness,
> and you will come to know Yahweh. (2:20-22)

And now again in Micah:

---

[80] [Portions of this letter are quoted in Adler, "Aspects of Jung's Personality and Work," p. 14. Presumably Dr. Edinger had access to the original, which has not otherwise been published.—Ed.]

> They will hammer their swords into ploughshares,
> their spears into sickles.
> Nation will not lift sword against nation,
> there will be no more training for war.
> Each man will sit under his vine and his fig tree,
> with no one to trouble him. (4:3-4)

These descriptions all indicate that the Messianic age somehow involves a reconciliation of the opposites, whereby the conflict between animals that are normally enemies, and conflict between man and animals which are normally in conflict with each other, and conflict between man and man, and between man and God—all these various conflicts, all these various oppositions, will be resolved. This describes a state of totality in which the divisions of the psyche have been harmonized by consciousness of the whole. So, as I have indicated before, I consider the image of the Messiah and the Messianic age to signify psychologically the achievement of the Self, consciously realized.

According to legend, in the Messianic age there will be the great Messianic Banquet, as mentioned earlier, at which the flesh of Behemoth and Leviathan will be eaten.[81] In other words, the primordial psyche will be transformed, humanized, in the process of being consciously assimilated.

According to one final image, in the Messianic age a new Torah will be taught and the dissociation between heaven and hell will be healed. Here is how it is described in a Midrash:

> The Holy One, blessed be He, will sit in the Garden of Eden and expound [the Torah] . . . . which He will give them through the Messiah. . . .
>
> In that hour the Holy One, blessed be He, takes the keys of Gehenna [hell] and, in front of all the pious, gives them to Michael and Gabriel [the archangels], and says to them: "Go and open the gates of Gehenna, and bring them up from Gehenna." . . .
>
> . . . And Gabriel and Michael stand over them [the wicked] in that hour, and wash them, and anoint them with oil, and heal them of the wounds of Gehenna, and clothe them in beautiful and good garments, and take them by their hand, and bring them before the Holy One, blessed be He.[82]

That is a good image with which to end our discussion of the Old Testament prophets.

---

[81] Above, pp. 29ff.

[82] In Patai, *The Messiah Texts,* pp. 252f.

Publisher's Tribute to Edward F. Edinger

The world is full of unconscious people—those who don't know why they do what they do. Edward F. Edinger did as much as anyone I know to correct this situation. To my mind, he was as true to Jung as one can be. Like Marie-Louise von Franz, he was a classic Jungian, pure and simple, by which I mean he took Jung's message to heart and amplified it according to his own talents. In a review of von Franz's biography, *C.G. Jung: His Myth in Our Time,* he described her as "a true spiritual daughter of Jung, a carrier of the pure Jungian elixir." Well, Dr. Edinger was a true spiritual son of Jung.

For those who find Jung himself tough going, Edinger has been the preeminent interpreter for more than thirty years. In lectures, books, tapes and videos, he has masterfully presented the distilled essence of Jung's work, illuminating its relevance to both collective and individual psychology.

After Inner City published his book *The Creation of Consciousness* in 1984, we enjoyed a warm working relationship. I visited him a couple of times at his home in Los Angeles, and sent him copies of each new Inner City title as it was published. He always responded quickly with a handwritten letter giving his considered opinion. Of course, not everything we published was his cup of tea, but he respected my choice of manuscripts as deriving from my own process of individuation: where my energy, at that time, wanted to go.

Every year or two Dr. Edinger offered Inner City Books a new manuscript. We took them all because they were good meaty stuff. Clean, crisp writing, no padding, no nonsense, no blather. They fit perfectly with our self-professed mandate "to promote the understanding and practical application" of Jung's work. More than that, their content has kept me psychologically alert. We are proud now to have thirteen Edinger titles under our wing, and thanks to the devoted energy of others there will soon be more.

Personally, I loved the man. I feel privileged and fortunate indeed to be in a position to keep his work and spirit alive, to the benefit of all those who strive to become more conscious.

Daryl Sharp

Bibliography

Adler, Gerhard. "Aspects of Jung's Personality and Work." In *Psychological Perspectives,* vol. 6, no. 1 (Spring 1975).

Alighieri, Dante. *The Divine Comedy.* Trans. John Ciardi. New York: W.W. Norton, 19770.

The Apostolic Fathers, vol. 2. Ed. Kirsopp Lake. Cambridge: Harvard University Press, 1913.

Burkert, Walter. *Greek Religion.* Trans. John Raffan. Cambridge: Harvard University Press, 1985.

Doré, Gustav. *The Doré Bible Illustrations.* New York: Dover Publications, 1974.

_____. *The Doré Illustrations for Dante's Divine Comedy.* New York: Dover Publications, 1976.

Edinger, Edward F. *The Aion Lectures: Exploring the Self in Jung's* Aion. Ed. Deborah A. Wesley. Toronto: Inner City Books, 1996.

_____. Anatomy of the Psyche: Alchemical Symbolism in Psychotherapy. La Salle, IL: Open Court, 1985.

_____. *The Bible and the Psyche: Individuation Symbolism in the Old Testament.* Toronto: Inner City Books, 1986.

_____. *Ego and Archetype: Individuation and the Religious Function of the Psyche.* Boston: Shambhala Publications, 1992.

_____. *Melville's Moby-Dick: An American Nekyia.* Toronto: Inner City Books, 1995.

_____. *The Mysterium Lectures: A Journey through C.G. Jung's* Mysterium Coniunctionis. Ed. Joan Dexter Blackmer. Toronto: Inner City Books, 1995.

_____. *Transformation of the God-Image: An Elucidation of Jung's* Answer to Job. Ed. Lawrence W. Jaffe. Toronto: Inner City Books, 1992.

Emerson, Ralph Waldo. *Essays.* New York: Harper and Row, 1951.

_____. *Nature.* Boston: Beacon Press, 1985.

Ginsberg, Louis. *Legends of the Bible.* Philadelphia: Jewish Publication Society of America, 1956.

Gubitz, Myron B. "Amelek: The Eternal Adversary." In *Psychological Perspectives,* vol. 8, no. 1 (Spring 1977).

Hegel, G.W.H. *The Philosophy of History.* Trans. J. Sibree. New York: Dover Publications, 1956.

Hobbes, Thomas. *Leviathan.* Oxford, UK: Clariden Press, 1909.

Jerusalem Bible. Garden City, NY: Doubleday and Co., 1966.

Jonas, Hans. *The Gnostic Religion.* Boston: Beacon Press, 1958.

Jung, C.G. *The Collected Works* (Bollingen Series XX). 20 vols. Trans. R.F.C. Hull. Ed. H. Read, M. Fordham, G. Adler, Wm. McGuire. Princeton: Princeton University Press, 1953-1979.

_____. *Letters* (Bollingen Series XCV). 2 vols. Trans. R.F.C. Hull. Ed. Gerhard Adler and Aniela Jaffé. Princeton: Princeton University Press, 1975.

_____. *Memories, Dreams, Reflections.* Ed. Aniela Jaffé. New York: Random House, 1963.

_____. *The Visions Seminars.* 2 vols. Zurich: Spring Publications, 1976.

Kaufmann, Walter. *Nietzsche: Philosopher, Psychologist, Antichrist.* Princeton: Princeton University Press, 1974.

_____. ed. and trans. *The Gay Science.* New York: Vintage Books, 1974.

_____, ed. *The Portable Nietzsche.* New York: Penguin Books, 1982.

King James Bible. HyperBible: The Computerized Chain Reference Tool for Windows. CD version 3.03.

Kirsch, James. *The Reluctant Prophet.* Los Angeles: Sherbourne Press, 1973.

Kluger, Rivkah Schärf. "The Image of the Marriage between God and Israel." In *Spring 1950.*

Kushner, Lawrence. *Sefer OTiYOT (The Book of Letters): A Mystical Alef-bait.* New York: Harper and Row, 1975.

Living Bible. Wheaton, IL: Tyndale House Publishers, 1971.

Neumann, Erich. *The Origins and History of Consciousness* (Bollingen Series XLII). Trans. R.F.C. Hull. Princeton: Princeton University Press, 1954.

New American Bible. New York: Thomas Nelson Publishers, 1971.

New King James Bible. HyperBible: The Computerized Chain Reference Tool for Windows. CD version 3.03.

Paracelsus. *The Hermetic and Alchemical Writings of Paracelsus.* Ed. and trans. A.E. Waite. New Hyde Park, NY: University Books, 1967.

Patai, Raphael. *The Messiah Texts.* Detroit: Wayne State University Press, 1979.

Scholem, Gershom G. *Major Trends in Jewish Mysticism.* New York: Schocken Books, 1974.

_____, *The Messianic Idea in Judaism.* Trans. Michael A. Meyer and Hillel Halkin. New York: Schocken Books, 1971.

Untermeyer, Louis, ed. *A Concise Treasury of Great Poems: English and American.* Toronto: Simon and Schuster of Canada (Cardinal ed.), 1968.

von Franz, Marie-Louise, ed. with commentary. *Aurora Consurgens: A Document Attributed to Thomas Aquinas on the Problem of Opposites in Alchemy.* 2nd ed. Toronto: Inner City Books, 2000.

Wilhelm, Richard, trans. *The I Ching or Book of Changes* (Bollingen Series XIX). 3rd ed. Trans. into English by Cary F. Baynes. Princeton: Princeton University Press, 1967.

Index

Also by Edward F. Edinger in this series

Prices and Payment in $US (except in Canada, $Cdn)

THE PSYCHE IN ANTIQUITY
Book 1: Early Greek Philosophy. ISBN 0-919123-86-4. (1999) 128 pp. $16
Book 2: Gnosticism and Early Christianity. ISBN 0-919123-87-2. (1999) 160 pp. $16

THE AION LECTURES: Exploring the Self in Jung's *Aion*
ISBN 0-919123-72-4. (1996) 208 pp. **30 illustrations** $18

MELVILLE'S MOBY-DICK: An American Nekyia
ISBN 0-919123-70-8. (1995) 160 pp. $16

THE MYSTERIUM LECTURES
A Journey Through Jung's *Mysterium Coniunctionis*
ISBN 0-919123-66-X. (1995) 352 pp. **90 illustrations** $25

THE MYSTERY OF THE CONIUNCTIO
Alchemical Image of Individuation
ISBN 0-919123-67-8. (1994) 112 pp. **48 illustrations** $16

GOETHE'S FAUST: Notes for a Jungian Commentary
ISBN 0-919123-44-9. (1990) 112 pp. $16

THE CHRISTIAN ARCHETYPE
A Jungian Commentary on the Life of Christ
ISBN 0-919123-27-9. (1987) 144 pp. **34 illustrations** $16

THE BIBLE AND THE PSYCHE
Individuation Symbolism in the Old Testament
ISBN 0-919123-23-6. (1986) 176 pp. $18

ENCOUNTER WITH THE SELF
A Jungian Commentary on William Blake's *Illustrations of the Book of Job*
ISBN 0-919123-21-X. (1986) 80 pp. **22 illustrations** $15

THE CREATION OF CONSCIOUSNESS
Jung's Myth for Modern Man
ISBN 0-919123-13-9. (1984) 128 pp. **10 illustrations** $16

Discounts: any 3-5 books, 10%; 6-9 books, 20%; 10 or more, 25%
Add Postage/Handling: 1-2 books, $3; 3-4 books, $5; 5-9 books, $10; 10 or more, free

Ask for **Jung at Heart** newsletter and free Catalogue of **over 90 titles**

INNER CITY BOOKS
Box 1271, Station Q, Toronto, ON M4T 2P4, Canada

Tel. (416) 927-0355 / Fax (416) 924-1814 / E-mail: icb@inforamp.net